THE VIKINGS AND THEIR AGE

COMPANIONS TO MEDIEVAL STUDIES
series editor: Paul Edward Dutton

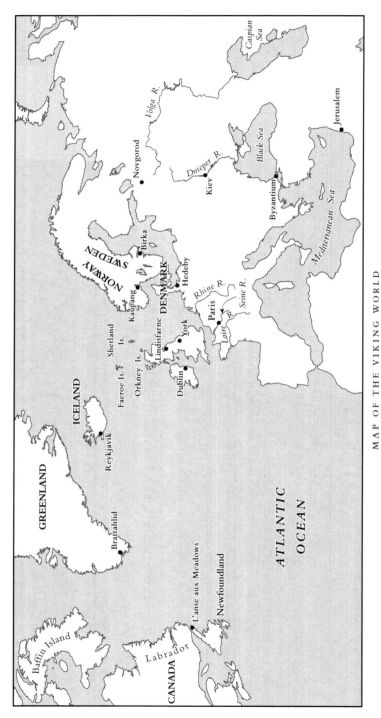

MAP OF THE VIKING WORLD

THE VIKINGS AND THEIR AGE

by Angus A. Somerville
and R. Andrew McDonald

UNIVERSITY OF TORONTO PRESS

LIBRARY AND ARCHIVES CANADA CATALOGUING IN PUBLICATION

Somerville, Angus A., 1943–
    The Vikings and their age / Angus A. Somerville and R. Andrew McDonald.

(Companions to medieval studies series ; v. 1)
Includes bibliographical references and index.
Also issued in electronic format.

ISBN 978-1-4426-0522-0 (paperback)
ISBN 978-1-4426-0762-0 (cloth)

    1. Vikings. 2. Civilization, Viking. 3. Vikings—Sources.
I. McDonald, Russell Andrew, 1965– II. Title. III. Series: Companions to medieval studies series ; v. 1

DL65.S64 2013   948'022   C2012-908017-9

We welcome comments and suggestions regarding any aspect of our publications—please feel free to contact us at news@utphighereducation.com or visit our Internet site at www.utppublishing.com.

North America	UK, Ireland, and continental Europe
5201 Dufferin Street	NBN International
North York, Ontario, Canada, M3H 5T8	Estover Road, Plymouth, PL6 7PY, UK
	ORDERS PHONE: 44 (0) 1752 202301
2250 Military Road	ORDERS FAX: 44 (0) 1752 202333
Tonawanda, New York, USA, 14150	ORDERS E-MAIL: enquiries@nbninternational.com

ORDERS PHONE: 1–800–565–9523
ORDERS FAX: 1–800–221–9985
ORDERS E-MAIL: utpbooks@utpress.utoronto.ca

Every effort has been made to contact copyright holders; in the event of an error or omission, please notify the publisher.

The University of Toronto Press acknowledges the financial support for its publishing activities of the Government of Canada through the Canada Book Fund.

Printed in Canada

For our families

CONTENTS

ILLUSTRATIONS

Photos

Maps

TEXT BOXES

ACKNOWLEDGMENTS

We are grateful to the University of Toronto Press for inviting us to write this book. In particular we thank Natalie Fingerhut for once again guiding the book through the press with professionalism and patience, and Paul Dutton for invaluable comments and expert guidance. As with *The Viking Age: A Reader,* the book would not have been possible without the many students who have populated our courses on Viking history and Old Norse over the years at Brock University, and we hope that this little book may prove useful to future students in those classes. We are grateful to Loris Gasparotto for producing the maps, and to Margaret Stephenson and Candice Bogdanski for permission to use two of their images. As ever, our biggest debt is to our families, who continue to live with the Vikings: Barbara, Anna, and Clare; Jacqueline, Emma, and Colin.

INTRODUCTION

This book provides a brief introduction to the Viking Age and to the results of scholarship on the period. *The Vikings and Their Age* relies heavily on the same sources and resources as our volume *The Viking Age: A Reader,* which presented a variety of documents relating to the Vikings and the Viking Age. While this book provides references to relevant passages in the *Reader,* it is itself a guide to the historical and scholarly issues involved in the study of the Viking Age. It contextualizes the material of the *Reader* so that students may approach the documents that the *Reader* contains with a better understanding of how and where they fit into the broader picture of the Vikings and their time.

We begin with a brief overview of the chronology and major themes of the Viking Age in chapter 1, while chapter 2 does the same for Viking society, pagan religion and mythology, and the conversion to Christianity. Chapter 3 contains brief biographies of several interesting and significant figures, both to illustrate the breadth and diversity of the Viking experience and to provide additional information on some of the characters who crop up frequently in the *Reader.*

Any study of the Vikings requires a multi-disciplinary approach, so we provide insights and evidence from disciplines such as archaeology, philology, and linguistics. However, our main focus is on the written record. Chapter 4, therefore, includes a sampling of the different types of documentary evidence available, as well as some advice on how to read and analyze such a diverse array of source materials. Chapter 5 offers a case study in reading and interpreting a short document pertinent to the Viking Age. The Afterword steps back to provide some brief thoughts on what impact the Vikings had on medieval Europe, and the volume concludes with what we hope are some useful reflective aids and tools for students.

OUR USE OF THE TERM *VIKING*

The usefulness of the term is the subject of debate among academics, some of whom avoid its use entirely because of its infrequent use in the Viking Age (see chapter 1). We employ the term in its widely accepted sense as a descriptor for the peoples of Scandinavia in the period from the late eighth to the eleventh centuries, not only for those who, by undertaking seaborne raiding, were Vikings in the contemporary sense of the word (see Glossary). The terms *Norse, Norsemen,* and *Northmen* are used interchangeably throughout.

A WORD ON VIKING NAMES

The Vikings did not use family names or surnames. Individuals were designated by a given name followed by a patronymic or, less commonly, a matronymic. A patronymic was formed by taking the father's name and adding the suffix *-son* or *-dóttir* (son/daughter). Thus, Egil Skallagrimsson is Egil, the son of Skallagrim, and his brother is Thorolf Skallagrimsson. Egil's son is Thorstein Egilsson, and his daughter is Thorgerd Egilsdóttir. (In this text, following the practice of the *Reader,* we use the anglicized form Egilsdaughter.) Matronymics could also be used, especially in cases where the father died young. The Orcadian chieftain Svein Asleifarson (see Chapter 3) illustrates this form; his mother was Asleif. The system is still used in Iceland today, where telephone directories list individuals by first names.

Identification by epithet is also common. Sometimes the meaning of the epithet is puzzling, as with the Danish king Harald Bluetooth or Ivar the Boneless, one of the leaders of the Great Heathen Army that invaded England in the 860s. Egil Skallagrimsson's grandfather, Ulf, was known as Kveldulf (Evening-Wolf) because he was thought to be a shape-shifter who became a wolf by night. Nicknames and epithets imprint some individuals from the Viking Age indelibly on our memories: Asgeir Scatter-Brain, Aud the Deep-Minded, Eirik Ale-Lover, Eystein Foul-Fart, Eyvind the Plagiarist, Gunnlaug Serpent Tongue, Halfred the Troublesome Poet, Olvir Child-Sparer, Sigtrygg Silken-Beard, Thorbjorg Ship-Breast, and, perhaps topping them all...Thorgils Mound-Shitter.

A NOTE ON LANGUAGE

As is usual, the names of persons are anglicized: Egill appears as Egil, and Guðrún as Gudrun.

Only two symbols from Old Norse are likely to cause confusion on the rare occasions when they are used here: Ð, ð (eth), pronounced 'th' as in *that*; Þ, þ (thorn), pronounced 'th' as in *thin*.

CONVENTIONS

The following abbreviations are adopted throughout:

BCE/CE   Before the Common Era/Common Era (now widely used
          as an alternative to BC and AD dating; the dates are
          identical, however, in both systems)

ca   *circa*   about; approximately (used where dates are inexact)

fl.   *floruit*   flourished (used where precise dates of an individual's life
          are uncertain, to indicate the main period in which that
          individual was active)

r.   reigned   used for reign dates of kings

CHAPTER ONE

THE VIKING AGE: AN OVERVIEW

WHO WERE THE VIKINGS?

In Old Norse, the language of the Scandinavian peoples of the Viking Age, a Viking was a sea-borne raider, and to go a-viking was to undertake sea-borne raiding. The word is a job description, but it applied only to a small minority of the population. It did not apply to women, children, slaves or others who did not undertake raiding. Being a Viking was a part-time job, since Viking expeditions were undertaken seasonally by small farmers, fishermen, merchants, chieftains, and aristocrats as a means of supplementing their income and winning fame. It was not until the nineteenth century that the term passed into common English usage, where it has generally come to be used as a descriptor for the peoples of Scandinavia in the period from the late eighth to the eleventh centuries, not just for those who undertook sea-borne raiding and were therefore Vikings in the contemporary sense of the word.

The term "Viking," though it existed in the early Middle Ages, was seldom used in contemporary sources. The Anglo-Saxons used the word *wicingas*, but those who suffered at their hands used a variety of terms to describe them. Common designations in contemporary European and Insular (that is, from the British Isles) sources include the terms Northmen, Norsemen, Danes, foreigners, pirate-ship men, pagans, and heathens. In the east, to the Byzantines they were known as *Rūs* and *Varangians*; to the Muslims they were Magians (*al-Majus*) or Rūs (*al-Rus*). All of these terms are of uncertain etymology.

WHEN AND WHAT WAS THE VIKING AGE?

The label "Viking Age" is commonly applied to several hundred years of European history between the late eighth century and the middle of the eleventh century, when Viking expansion represents an important theme in European history. The years 793 to 1066 are frequently cited as defining the period, but these dates are subject to debate and are not precise markers of the beginning and end of the period.

The reach of the Vikings extended to a vast geographical area, from the Arctic Circle in the north to the Mediterranean in the south; from Newfoundland in the west to Constantinople and Azerbaijan in the east. Such geographical and temporal scope produced a remarkably varied Viking culture.

The concept of a "Viking Age" is a modern one, invented by Scandinavian scholars, principally archaeologists, in the second half of the nineteenth century, just as the concept of the "Middle Ages" is an invention of the Northern Italian Renaissance. People in the Middle Ages did not think of themselves as living in the middle of anything; neither did early medieval Scandinavians nor their European neighbors regard themselves as living in a "Viking Age." The Viking Age is an artificial construct used to assist in the conceptualization of history, a point to bear in mind with regard to disputes concerning the beginning and end of the period.

VIKING *AGE* OR VIKING *AGES*?

Indeed, the concept of a monolithic "Viking Age" breaks down under close scrutiny. The Viking Age was a time of dynamic and complex change, with several phases of activity spanning several hundred years. The small-scale, unorganized, predatory raiding parties of the late eighth and early ninth centuries gave way to larger, better-organized armies by the middle of the ninth century; the fact that it is only from the middle of the ninth century that we know something about the names of individual leaders of armies and fleets is itself significant. Settlement also began to occur by the middle of the ninth century, first in the British Isles, later on the Continent. The period from 981 to 1016 in England saw highly organized royal expeditions intent upon exacting tribute and achieving political conquest. Within Scandinavia a plurality of local and regional chieftaincies and kingdoms coalesced into the unitary kingdoms of Denmark, Norway, and Sweden. Outside Scandinavia, strong political entities ruled by Scandinavian dynasties took shape. Intensified commercial and diplomatic relations with Britain and Europe brought contact with Christianity, and this was the age when the cross went north into Scandinavia. The conversion of the Scandinavians is an important theme that spans the entire Viking Age. In fact, the earliest missionaries to the north had probably arrived before the first raiders landed at Lindisfarne in 793, and the German cleric Adam of Bremen was still reporting scandalous pagan practices at Uppsala in Sweden in the late eleventh century. By the time the age drew to a close, the Scandinavians had changed the face of Europe—and had, in turn, been changed by it. To understand how this happened, it might be more useful to think in terms of several Viking *Ages* rather than a single Viking *Age*. Before turning to the development of these Viking Ages, it is necessary to consider the Scandinavian roots of the Vikings, the causes of the Viking expansion, and the naval technology that made the Vikings lords of the seas.

SCANDINAVIAN ROOTS

The people we call Vikings originated in modern Norway, Sweden, and Denmark, though these political divisions only came into existence later in the Middle Ages. These countries, forming most of modern Scandinavia, cover an area of some 800,000 km² in northern Europe, stretching about 2,000 km from the Danish-German frontier to Cape North in Norway, well above the Arctic Circle. Not surprisingly, given the size of the region, it exhibits great diversity in landscape and environment. Norway is characterized by a long coastline deeply indented with steep-sided fjords, numerous offshore islands, and mountainous terrain (about one-quarter of the country comprises land over 1000 m in elevation). Denmark is low lying, its highest point only 175 m above sea level, with a long coastline, many islands, and a temperate climate. Denmark is blessed, too, with the most fertile soils in Scandinavia; Norway has hardly any, and today only about three per cent of it is arable. The sea has always played a vital role in the Scandinavian economy and society: no point in Denmark is more than 75 km from the water, and the name of Norway is derived from the long sea-road running down its northwestern coast, the "North Way." The size and varied environment of Scandinavia mean that diversity rather than unity is one of its defining characteristics; archaeologists in particular have stressed the regionalization of early medieval Scandinavian material culture.

Despite the modern tendency to think of all of the early inhabitants of Scandinavia as "Vikings," the region was home to a number of different peoples. Ninth-century texts distinguish Norwegians or Northmen (a term sometimes used to describe all the inhabitants of Scandinavia), Danes, the Svear, and the Götar. They were not politically united and spoke different forms of

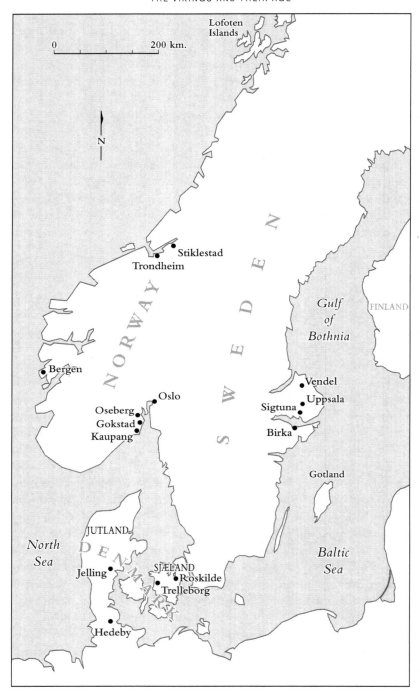

MAP I.I **Scandinavia in the Viking Age**

PHOTO I.I   The Norwegian Environment. Much of Norway comprises rugged mountains and deeply indented fjords with sparse arable land: a fjord scene in Sognefjord.
(Photo by C. Bogdanski)

North Germanic. Another group of people inhabiting the northernmost Arctic
and sub-Arctic regions of Scandinavia were the Lapps or Sami. These people
were primarily hunter-gatherers and spoke a Finno-Ugrian language. They
were not Vikings, although they certainly interacted in a variety of ways with
the other inhabitants of Scandinavia.

Settlement patterns show continuity from earlier periods of the Scandinavian Iron Age into the Viking Age. Most settlement was rural, and most
Scandinavians, both before and during the Viking Age, were farmers, living in
relatively small settlements that varied in size, layout, building techniques, and
resources depending upon their location. Danish settlements were generally
larger and more productive than those in Sweden and Norway, although bar-
ley, oats, and rye could be cultivated in parts of northern Scandinavia. Variation also existed between the farms of large magnates and those lower in the
social hierarchy. Smaller settlements might have had only two or three buildings, while more substantial ones had more, with larger domestic buildings as
well as stables, workshops, and storage buildings. Stock rearing was generally
vital to the Scandinavian way of life, with cattle, horses, sheep, and goats being
particularly important. Fishing, hunting, and trapping supplemented agricultural resources, particularly in northern Scandinavia. Scandinavian settlements
of the eighth century have been characterized as versatile and self-sufficient.

PHOTO I.2   Reconstructed Icelandic Commonwealth Period (930–1262) House at Stöng in Thjorsardalur. The original was covered by ash during an eruption of Mount Hekla in 1104. The ash preserved material features that made this reconstruction possible. The construction material is turf with a wooden frame. (Photo by R.A. McDonald)

The main building type throughout Scandinavia from the Bronze Age was the three-aisled longhouse, in which pairs of posts supported the roof. These houses varied in size and were divided into several rooms; large houses often had a stable, kitchen, storerooms, and space for entertaining and living. In some regions the longhouse became wider and taller during the Viking Age. In other regions a new type developed, with a single aisle and roof-supporting walls.

Scandinavian society remained essentially rural and agricultural throughout the Viking Age, but the eighth century witnessed the development of urban communities characterized by craft production and trade. Urbanization in Scandinavia occurred in two waves, the first of which belongs to the second half of the eighth century, the second to the decades around 1000. The earliest urban center to develop was Birka in Sweden (ca 750), strategically situated astride transportation and communication routes on a small island in Lake Mälaren. Three more towns then developed in Danish-controlled areas at Ribe (ca 790s), Kaupang (ca 800) in Vestfold in modern-day Norway, and Hedeby (ca 808) near modern Schleswig in Germany, all situated at strategic hubs for trade. Only a few thousand inhabitants may have lived in these towns, perhaps 10 per cent of the total population, but their economic, social, and political significance was disproportionate to their size. These four towns were deserted or lost status (Ribe ca 850, Kaupang ca 930, Birka ca 970, Hedeby ca 1060) and new urban communities developed in the years around 1000. The causes of these changes are complex and not fully understood.

Seasonal marketplaces, described as non-urban places of trade and craft, have also been identified. Whereas towns were permanent communities, marketplaces were occupied seasonally. Some were large, while others were small; some are found in close association with the estates of kings or magnates. Some towns, like Ribe and Kaupang, may have developed from seasonal marketplaces.

The development of these urban and commercial centers is linked to high-status individuals at the apex of the Scandinavian social hierarchy, and it is believed that they developed under the protection, control, and sponsorship of regional kings or chieftains, probably inspired by European (especially Carolingian) models. The uniformity of street plans and the layout of property boundaries and plots, as well as the close proximity of royal manors to the urban foundations at Birka and Kaupang, all suggest powerful patronage. Frankish annals indicate that the Danish king played a role in establishing Hedeby.

The consolidation of power by such men is evident in the construction of monuments such as the 14-km-long earthwork known as the Danevirke at the foot of the Jutland Peninsula (ca 737; later rebuilt several times) and the timber-lined canal at Kanhave (ca 726; later repaired), as well as in the high-status cemeteries at Uppsala in Sweden and at Borre in Norway. Denmark may have been a unified kingdom under a single king in the eighth century; the Danish king, Godfred, was an opponent of Charlemagne and is frequently mentioned in Frankish sources. In central Sweden the pre-Christian kingdoms are regarded as possessing fairly sophisticated political organizations. Nevertheless, with the possible exception of Denmark, unified Scandinavian kingdoms did not exist at the dawn of the Viking Age (see chapter 2).

BOX 1.1   *Borg in Lofoten: A Chieftain's Dwelling in Arctic Norway*

In 1981, a Norwegian farmer at Borg in the Lofoten Islands of northern Norway spotted unusual charcoal deposits, charred stones, and objects while ploughing. Excavation revealed the remains of several buildings and many artifacts. A large house-site turned out to be the remains of two buildings, one constructed on top of the other. The earlier structure was dated to the fifth or sixth century and was pulled down in the seventh century, when the larger structure was built. At 83 m in length, this is the largest dwelling so far discovered anywhere in the Viking world. Both buildings were three-aisled wooden houses with large wooden posts to support the roof. The later house had five rooms and five entrances, with nearly half the total length (33 m) given over to the substantial byre (shelter for cattle) at one end, which would have accommodated many animals; it is a house fit for a chieftain. The site's high status is also evident from the size of the central room (120 m²) as well as its associated artifacts: gold objects, fragments of glass vessels, pottery, tools, and equipment. Five gold foil plaques, possibly ritual objects, remind us that both domestic and ritual functions took place in the halls of these longhouses. The artifacts testify to the wide-ranging contacts of the inhabitants, but farming and fishing remained the basis of the community's subsistence.

CAUSES OF THE VIKING EXPANSION

The Scandinavians themselves left no contemporary explanations for the causes of Viking expansion, although their descendants in Iceland regarded the tyrannical reign of the Norwegian king Harald Finehair (ca 880–ca 930) as a catalyst for the migration of disgruntled, freedom-loving chieftains and their followers. For contemporary European and Byzantine writers, the answer was clear: the Viking attacks were divine punishment for the sins of the times.

Lacking contemporary Scandinavian texts, modern scholars have postulated many reasons for Viking expansion, but few command universal support. The causes of the expansion continue to be debated vigorously, and this problem constitutes one of the most challenging in the field of Viking studies.

Overpopulation and land hunger in the Scandinavian homelands are frequently cited as explanations for Scandinavian expansion, although there is some skepticism about this. Settlements in early medieval Scandinavia were diverse in size and nature; some certainly shared in the expansion that characterized Europe generally toward the end of the first millennium, but others demonstrate little change from the Roman Iron Age right through to the late Middle Ages. The chronology of settlement expansion is also problematic: in some instances this is now thought to have occurred *during* the Viking Age rather than before it. The structure of the population in early medieval Scandinavia may have been more important than its overall size; selective female infanticide and a preference for sons over daughters in a competitive political environment may have led large numbers of young men to seek an opportunity to win wealth and reputation by undertaking Viking expeditions abroad (Barrett 2008). A strong argument against the hypothesis that land hunger drove the Viking diaspora is that the main aim of Scandinavian raiders in the first half of the ninth century was plunder rather than land; settlement began some 50 years after the earliest recorded raids.

Another popular explanation, developed from the sagas of Icelanders, views the consolidation of political authority in Norway by Harald Finehair as a spur to migration. This foundation-story was firmly impressed in the minds of Icelandic saga writers of the thirteenth and fourteenth centuries, and it may indeed have played a role in the colonization and unique socio-political development of Iceland. Harald's reign belongs to the end of the ninth century and the start of the tenth, far too late to account for the initial expansion from the Scandinavian homelands that commenced in the late eighth century. Frankish sources hint at eighth-century political changes in Scandinavia, particularly in Denmark. These changes may have contributed to Scandinavian expansion. Certainly, some of the earliest Danish "Vikings" active on the Continent seem to have been political exiles.

A further suggestion is that the aggressive expansion of the Carolingian empire of Charlemagne (r. 768–814) fueled an ideologically driven struggle between this Christian empire and the pagan Scandinavian world. According to this view, sometimes called the "pagan reaction hypothesis," Viking raids were essentially in self-defense. But Scandinavian paganism lacked aggression and intolerance, and in any event Scandinavian society at the outset of the Viking Age was hardly unified enough to launch coordinated attacks on western Christendom. This explanation is more satisfactory in a Danish context than for all Scandinavia, and it does not seem to be applicable to the raids on the British Isles.

Other explanations emphasize the close connections between piracy and trade, suggesting that pre-existing trade networks of the eighth century as well as Scandinavian knowledge of European wealth invited the transition from commercial activity to raiding later in the century. Substantial quantities of continental glassware and pottery were reaching Scandinavia before the Viking Age and are interpreted as evidence of peaceful trade. It has also been pointed out that piracy was never entirely absent from the North Sea area in the early Middle Ages. A related explanation argues that a shortage of silver from the east ignited an early medieval silver-rush as alternate supplies were sought. Both ideas remain the subject of debate.

What might be called the "heroic nature" of late Iron Age Scandinavian society should also be considered. This was a society geared for war, with deep-seated beliefs in concepts of honor and fatalism. The quest for fame was paramount. While not unique to Scandinavia or the Viking Age, such beliefs might help explain why so many Viking Age Scandinavians were willing to embark on highly risky enterprises (Price 2002).

No single explanation will suffice for such a complex and dynamic phenomenon as Viking expansion. Recent scholarship has emphasized the need to distinguish between long- and short-term developments when searching for the causes of the expansion, and it has also been asked whether the appearance of Scandinavians as raiders around the coasts of Europe and the British Isles was indeed as sudden an event as we have frequently been led to believe (Simek 2004; Barrett 2008).

Other factors that facilitated the Viking expansion could be considered as catalysts rather than as direct causes. Some of these were environmental, others technological. It has, for instance, been frequently observed that the Viking Age overlaps significantly with the Medieval Warm Period (MWP) or Little Climatic Optimum, when climatic conditions were generally more favorable for maritime travel and exploration than in preceding and following eras. The effects of the MWP were particularly significant in the North Atlantic and helped bring about the exploration and colonization of Iceland and Greenland; the climatic downturn of the late Middle Ages has figured prominently in discussions about the demise of the Norse Greenland colonies. Disagreement about the precise dating and nature of the MWP means that its role in facilitating Viking expansion remains contentious.

VIKING SHIPS: A CATALYST OF THE VIKING AGE

The high level of naval technology achieved by the Vikings also encouraged their expansion. Viking ship technology should be regarded not as a cause of the Viking Age, but rather as a necessary prerequisite for Viking expansion. Knowledge of Viking ships is derived from several sources. Documentary and iconographic material is important, but the principal source is surviving ships and parts of ships of varying sizes and designs that have been excavated since the mid-1800s throughout the regions that were settled by Scandinavians.

Viking ships were the result of centuries of development that can be traced in the remains of vessels such as the Hjortspring "war canoe" (ca 350 BCE, Denmark), the Nydam boat (ca 400 CE, Denmark), and the Kvalsund ship (ca 700 CE, Norway). The shape and size of Viking vessels varied according to the function they performed, but all shared some characteristics. They were built using a method known as clinker building (or shell building), by which overlapping strakes (planks) were riveted together. This technique produced flexible, yet extremely sturdy ships that could be rowed or sailed; their shallow draft enabled them to beach easily for trade or for raiding. They had symmetrical, upturned stem and stern posts, and the top line of the planking was elegantly curved so that it was higher at the ends than amidships. A large steer board (steering oar) was usually attached at the right-hand rear of the vessel (the origin of the nautical term "starboard"). Warships tended to be longer and more slender than cargo vessels, which were rounder, broader, shorter, and sturdier, with a deeper draft. Warships could be rowed or sailed, while cargo vessels relied principally upon sail and had only a few oars for maneuvering.

Literary texts use several terms to distinguish different types of vessel. Large ocean-going merchant and cargo ships were called *knörrs* (ON *knörr*, pl. *knerrir*); these were the vessels that were used for the colonization of Iceland and Greenland. One of the ships raised from Roskilde fjord in Denmark in 1962 is believed to be a *knörr* (see below). The term *ferja* was used for smaller transport or fishing ships. The term *langskip* (longship) is a general term for a warship with 32 or more sets of oars. The size of these vessels was usually indicated by the number of places they had for rowers, and the ships were divided into lateral compartments called "rooms." King Olaf's "Long Serpent," for example, was said to have had 34 "rooms" (and thus 68 oars), which would have made it one of the largest vessels ever constructed. A 13-bencher, with 26 oars, was considered the smallest ship suitable for warfare. Other terms for warships include *skeið* (large warship, pl. *skeiðir*), *snekkja* (swift warship, pl. *snekkjur*), and *dreki* (dragon, pl. *drekar*)—the latter probably so named for the removable dragon heads and tails that were sometimes attached to its prows.

Gokstad and Oseberg Ships, Norway

Two well-preserved Viking ships from Gokstad and Oseberg, on the west side of Oslofjord in Norway, are significant sources of information about Viking ships of the ninth and early tenth centuries. The Gokstad ship was discovered in the summer of 1880, when a large mound was excavated on a farm at Gokstad. It contained the well-preserved remains of a Viking ship that had been used for the burial of an important chieftain ca 900. The burial chamber had been plundered in antiquity and contained no weapons or personal items, but the remains of at least 12 horses and six dogs, a peacock, household goods, beds, a sledge, three small boats, and decayed textiles (probably part of the sail) were found. The ship was removed from the mound, painstakingly preserved and reconstructed, and now resides in the Vikingskipshuset (Viking Ship Museum) at Bygdøy, Oslo. It was made of oak, except for the mast and planking, which were pine. It is nearly 24 m in length with a beam of 5.2 m, and has a keel made from a single piece of timber. The vessel has 16 oars to a side, and the oar ports have shutters that could be closed when the vessel was under sail. Sixty-four circular, black and yellow shields were also found, and these would have been arranged 32 per side along the gunwale of the ship (though they could not have been displayed when the ship was being rowed, as they blocked the oar ports). The Gokstad ship was a general-purpose, seagoing vessel, capable of being rowed or sailed, that would have had a crew of

PHOTO I.3   The Oseberg Ship. Built ca 815–820. Now in the Viking Ship Museum, Bygdøy, Oslo. (Photo courtesy of the Viking Ship Museum, Oslo)

PHOTO I.4   Norse Head, Carving from Oseberg Ship Burial. Norway, early ninth century. (Photo courtesy of the Viking Ship Museum, Oslo)

PHOTO I.5 **The Gokstad Ship. Built ca 890. Now in the Viking Ship Museum, Bygdøy, Oslo. (Photo courtesy of the Viking Ship Museum, Oslo)**

at least 34, i.e., 32 oarsmen, a helmsman, and a captain. It probably represents a type known as a *karvi*, a warship that is slightly smaller than a *langskip*.

In 1904 another Viking ship was excavated from a burial mound at Oseberg. This is the richest burial from the Viking Age in Scandinavia, yielding a well-preserved vessel and an astonishing array of artifacts, including a wagon, sledges, animal head posts of uncertain purpose, utensils, and textiles. The ship was built ca 815–820 and had been in use for some time before being used for the burial of a prominent woman ca 834. The burial chamber held two female skeletons, one of a woman between 50 and 60 years of age, the other between 20 and 30. At 21.5 m long and with 15 oars per side, the Oseberg ship was slightly smaller than the Gokstad ship, but, like the Gokstad, the Oseberg was a large, open ship, powered by sail and oar (a full set of oars survived), and was probably of the *karvi* type. But the Oseberg was not as seaworthy as the Gokstad: the sides are lower, there are no shutters for the oar ports, and the vessel is generally more lightly built. The Oseberg vessel and the grave goods were conserved and are now displayed at the Viking Ship Museum at Bygdøy, Oslo.

The Skuldelev Ships, Denmark

The Gokstad and Oseberg ships were long regarded as characteristic Viking vessels. That changed in 1962, when the remains of five ships were excavated from the bottom of Roskildefjord on Zealand in Denmark. Unlike the Gokstad and Oseberg ships, these had not been used for burials but had been deliberately scuttled in the eleventh century as part of a system of blockades to protect Roskilde. The Skuldelev vessels were not nearly so well preserved as the Gokstad and Oseberg ships: only about 25 per cent of the large warship was preserved, but 50 to 75 per cent of the other vessels remains. Whereas the Gokstad and Oseberg ships date to the ninth century, the Skuldelev ships belong to the eleventh and represent different types of vessel. Two of the Skuldelev ships (Skuldelev 1 and Skuldelev 3) are trading vessels, and the former, at about 16 m long and 4.5 m wide, probably belongs to the class of ocean-going trading ship known as a *knörr*. Skuldelev 3 was a small trading vessel 14 m in length that was more suited to coastal sailing. Both were powered principally by sail; the Skuldelev 1 trader had only two to four oars. Two of the Skuldelev vessels were warships, and one of them was spectacular: Skuldelev 2 was a long, slender warship about 30 m in length, with 30 pairs of oars and a crew of 65 to 70. Dendrochronology (a dating method using tree rings) has revealed that this vessel was built in Dublin ca 1042 using Irish timber. Skuldelev 2 probably belonged to a type of vessel known as a *skeið*, and judging by its size, it was clearly the ship of a great lord. Skuldelev 5 was a smaller warship, 17.5 m in length, with 13 pairs of oars; it is probably of the *snekkja* type. Skuldelev 6 was a fishing vessel of the *ferja* class. The Skuldelev ships illustrate the diversity of vessel types in use during the Viking Age: the remains of these vessels are on display at the Vikingeskibs Museet (Viking Ship Museum) in Roskilde, Denmark. (Note that, for reasons beyond the scope of this discussion, there is no Skuldelev 4.)

Since the 1980s, the Viking Ship Museum has constructed replicas of the vessels, using the tools and techniques of Viking Age shipwrights. This process has brought to light many significant characteristics of Viking ships. *Roar Edge* is a replica of the Skuldelev 3 trading vessel, and *Helge Ask* is a replica of the small warship Skuldelev 5. Most impressive of all is *Sea Stallion*, a replica of the Skuldelev 2 warship; in the summer of 2007 this vessel sailed over 1,200 nautical miles from Roskilde to Dublin.

Although the Gokstad, Oseberg, and Skuldelev ships are the most famous Viking ship finds, they are by no means unique. Other significant ships have been excavated in Denmark, at Ladby in the 1930s and from Hedeby harbor in 1953 and 1979, and new ship discoveries continue. In 1990, the partly eroded ship burial of a small rowing boat (*færing*) with the bodies of a middle-aged man, an elderly woman, and a young child was excavated on the island of Sanday in Orkney. In 1997, during expansion of the harbor of the Viking Ship Museum in Roskilde, archaeologists discovered—lying near the museum!—the remains of a massive Viking longship. Dated to 1025, at 35 m in length it is the longest of all known Viking ships and corroborates saga accounts of massive dragon ships.

"SUDDEN AND UNFORESEEN ATTACKS OF NORTHMEN":
THE FIRST VIKING AGE—RAIDING AND RECONNAISSANCE

The ninth-century *Anglo-Saxon Chronicle* describes what may be the earliest recorded Viking raids: in 787 (or 789), a ship of Northmen landed in the south of England and killed a king's officer, and on 8 June 793 the monastery on Lindisfarne (a tidal island off the northeast coast of England) was sacked. These are the first recorded raids, but there is some uncertainty about the extent of earlier Scandinavian activity around the Atlantic frontiers of Europe. Given the fragmentary nature of the evidence, we cannot be sure that the earliest recorded raids were the first. Whatever the case, Viking raiders are mentioned frequently in European and Insular texts from the end of the eighth and beginning of the ninth centuries. Irish annals record the first appearance of the Northmen in the islands off the west coast of Britain and in Ireland from 795, and in 799 there is the first reference to Viking activity on the Continent. By the 830s and 840s, Viking fleets had penetrated far inland up waterways such as the Shannon, Loire, Seine, and Rhine. By the 850s and 860s, some intrepid leaders had reached the Mediterranean and the Rhône River. Continental and Irish annals record a raiding expedition in the late 850s and early 860s in which some 60 ships, led by Bjorn Ironsides and Hastein, voyaged from the Loire down the coast of the Iberian peninsula and through the straits of Gibraltar to plunder in North Africa, the south coast of France, and Italy, before returning home, greatly depleted in numbers.

Such predatory sea-borne raids instilled fear, shock, and awe in contemporaries and have inspired modern historians to distinguish a "First Viking Age," or period of "reconnaissance" characterized by raiding and plundering, lasting from the 790s until about the middle of the ninth century, when raiding intensified and gave way to overwintering (setting up temporary winter-quarters) and eventually to settlement in different parts of Britain and Europe. We should note that Vikings raided and pillaged other Scandinavians as happily as they did Europeans. The Vikings were not united against Europe, just as Europe was not united against the Vikings.

Early Viking raids were relatively small-scale, hit-and-run affairs. Before 850, fleets of over 100 ships are rarely mentioned, but after that date the numbers increase, with references to 120, 150, 200, or 250 ships. The accuracy of these figures from contemporary sources has been the subject of much debate, but most agree that there was a change in the nature of raiding from the 830s. The earliest raids were probably the work of Northmen from the west coast of Norway, but Danes soon followed. Raiders targeted vulnerable coastal sites, particularly monasteries such as Lindisfarne, Iona, and Noirmoutier (see below and box 1.2), and coastal trading centers such as Hamwic (Southampton) and Dorestad on the Rhine.

Scandinavian raiders sought portable wealth and captives who could be ransomed or sold as slaves. Contemporary sources sometimes noted precise numbers of captives taken, and an annotation in an English gospel book (Stockholm Codex Aureus) indicates that it was ransomed from a heathen army "with pure gold" by a local nobleman and his wife. Churches and monasteries were targeted not because the Vikings were "anti-Christian," but because such places were centers of wealth and convenient sources of captives. It was in the Vikings' best interest *not* to destroy such places entirely, as they could be replenished and raided again. Raids were largely seasonal affairs, carried out in the summer months, after which the raiders would return home (or to bases established in the Shetland and Orkney Isles, although this is debated); the seasonal rhythm of raiding is exemplified in a description of the Viking lifestyle of the Orkney chieftain Svein Asleifarson (see chapter 3) in *The Saga of the Orkney Islanders* (*Orkneyinga saga*).

Early raiding may have been completely unexpected, as may be inferred from a letter written by Alcuin to King Athelred of Northumbria in 793, although it is doubtful that the Northmen were completely unknown at the dawn of the Viking Age, either in the waters around northern Britain or on the Continent. Nevertheless, the overall impression given by the sources is that the raids instilled shock, awe, and terror in contemporaries. Little wonder that some historians have regarded the Vikings as early medieval terrorists (see below).

The sack of Nantes, near the mouth of the Loire, in 843 was well documented by several independent contemporary sources and is a good example of a ninth-century raid. Northmen had been active on the Atlantic coast of France for decades before 843. A particular target was the monastery of Noirmoutier (located on a small island at the mouth of the Loire), a nexus of the salt and wine trade. The raid on Nantes occurred on the feast day of Saint John the Baptist, 24 June 843 (the significance of which will become clearer later); the attackers probably hailed from the Vestfold region of Norway. The townspeople were given warning of the approach of the fleet (numbering 67 ships, according to a slightly later writer) by the monks of the nearby monastery of Indre, who fled to the town with their treasure. The gates of the city were barred, but the ancient Gallo-Roman defenses of the town were no match for the Northmen, who stormed the walls and battered down the gates. The populace fled to the cathedral, possibly because it was the strongest building in the city, but even this offered no security: the Vikings smashed down the doors, broke the windows, and put many of the occupants to the sword. They did not kill everyone, however, and survivors were taken away to the nearby ships, since prisoners could be ransomed or sold as slaves. Five days later the raiders made their way downriver with loot from the city, ransoming their captives in the process. In this instance, we are not told how much was paid as ransom, or who paid it, but a few years earlier, in 841, the abbey of Saint Wandrille paid 26 pounds of silver to redeem 68 captives. Nor do we hear of how the captives were treated, though other contemporary accounts relate the sufferings of captives—hunger, thirst, psychological and physical abuse—and leave no doubt that falling into the hands of marauding Northmen could be a terrifying experience.

That the attack occurred on an important feast-day was not a coincidence, and other examples of carefully timed raids are to be found. Scandinavian raiders were well aware that attacking on religious festivals meant that they were likely to find larger numbers of potential captives assembled in one place; this not only reveals knowledge of the Christian calendar on the part of the Northmen, but also indicates that they possessed good intelligence about their targets. Contemporary chronicles and annals reveal other Viking tactics, including attacks at dawn and by night, as well as the use of trickery and deception.

The sack of Nantes also provides an important example of the development of the myth of the Vikings as no more than terrorists during the Middle Ages. Simon Coupland, an historian who has investigated the phenomenon, has demonstrated how exaggeration crept into later medieval accounts of the raid, sometimes flatly contradicting original contemporary accounts (2003, 192). By the eleventh century, for instance, it was reported that Bishop Gunhard was cut down in his cathedral during the climax of the celebration of the mass. The bishop was indeed killed, but he was slain while seeking refuge from the attackers. This shows one way in which tales of Viking savagery could grow in the telling.

BOX 1.2   *Iona and Noirmoutier: A Tale of Two Monasteries in the Viking Age*

....

Iona, in the Hebrides off Scotland's west coast, and Noirmoutier, at the mouth of the Loire River, were both tiny Atlantic islands with important monastic communities that were repeatedly raided by Vikings in the early Middle Ages. Their exposed locations along the western seaways made them easy targets for the sea-going Scandinavians, and their status as religious communities with venerable founders (Saint Columba, d. 597, for Iona and Saint Philibert, d. 685, for Noirmoutier) did not save them from non-Christian raiders who regarded them as easy sources of captives and portable wealth. Their contrasting histories during the Viking Age are illuminating.

The first recorded raid on Iona occurred in 795. In 802, the monastery was plundered and burned, and in 806, 68 members of the community were slain. In 825, the monk Blathmac was tortured and slain when he refused to reveal the hiding place of the relics of Saint Columba; his martyrdom was recorded in a Latin poem by the contemporary Carolingian scholar Walafrid Strabo (d. 849). Blathmac's martyrdom illustrates two key points: first, that even after 30 years of raiding, Iona still possessed items of value to the Northmen; and second, despite the building of a new monastery at Kells in Ireland in 807 (perhaps as a refuge for some members of the Iona community), the monastery endured. Indeed, although Iona lost some status after 849, when some relics of Saint Columba were transferred to Dunkeld in eastern Scotland, business probably continued more or less as usual through the rest of the Viking Age and beyond. In fact, Iona seems to have played an influential role in the conversion of Scandinavian settlers in the Hebrides from the mid-ninth century, and in 980 the defeated Norse king of Dublin, Olaf Cuarán, went to Iona on pilgrimage, ending his days there as a member of the monastic community. It was a fitting testimony to Iona's resilience and influence in the Viking Age.

Noirmoutier was situated at the center of the regional trade in salt and wine. Like Iona, it endured a succession of Viking raids from the end of the eighth century. Between 814 and 819, the monks of Saint Philibert constructed a church on the nearby mainland at Déas as a place of refuge, and for a while the community moved seasonally back and forth between the two sites, avoiding Noirmoutier during the summer when the Northmen were active on the waterways. In 836, after repeated raids, Noirmoutier was abandoned altogether and the relics of Saint Philibert were transferred to Déas. After Déas was pillaged and burned in 847, the monks were on the move again and relocated to Cunault in Anjou. In 858 they were able to retrieve the relics of Saint Philibert, and for nearly two decades they wandered from monastery to monastery, through Poitou and Auvergne, before settling at Tournus in Burgundy in 875, more than 300 miles from Noirmoutier. Unlike Iona, where the monastic community survived, Noirmoutier and Déas were largely forgotten; Déas was not resettled until the early eleventh century. The monks of Saint Philibert were not unique in their experience: the monks of Lindisfarne, for example, endured a similar experience between the abandonment of their monastery at Lindisfarne in 875 and their resettlement at Chester-le-Street in 883.

Ermentarius, a member of the monastic community, recorded the wanderings and tribulations of the monks of Saint Philibert in 863. His text, part of which is reproduced in chapter 5 as a document case study, provides a gripping and graphic account of the terror and devastation wrought by the Northmen in the Frankish kingdoms. It shows, too, how different orders of medieval society responded to Viking raids, and highlights the way in which the Northmen took advantage of divisions and disorganization within Francia.

The extent of Viking raiding and the political fragmentation of much of Europe and the British Isles in the early Middle Ages help explain the variety of responses to Viking raids. Major challenges to dealing with these assaults included the great mobility of Viking raiding parties (particularly in the first phase of the Viking Age), the relatively poor transportation and communication infrastructures throughout Europe, the difficulties of marshaling and mobilizing the manpower and resources required to keep the Vikings in check, and the complexities of contemporary politics that often not only prevented effective resistance but also sometimes actually made matters easier for the Vikings.

Military actions enjoyed varying degrees of success. Vikings were not invincible, and Scandinavian raiding parties could be, and were, defeated: Irish annals, for instance, record eight battles between Vikings and Irish in the years between 845 and 848, with the Vikings bested in seven of the eight encounters. Early medieval armies, however, were not generally geared for defensive duties, and the Vikings' mobility made them difficult to control. The Mercian king Offa (r. 757–796) ordered the strengthening of the coastal defenses of his kingdom against unnamed pirates in 796; the pirates were probably Scandinavian raiders. The Frankish king Charlemagne organized coast guards and fleets to protect his realm near the end of his reign. The construction or rebuilding of fortifications was one effective method of dealing with Viking raiding, and two well-known examples of public defenses organized by kings occurred in the west Frankish kingdom under Charles the Bald (r. 843–877) and in Wessex under Alfred (r. 871–899). Charles the Bald fortified bridges, towns, monasteries, and palaces against Viking attack. His fortified bridge at Pont de l'Arche near Pîtres on the Seine, begun in 862, is one of the most famous examples. It was designed to prevent Viking penetration up the Seine River and to protect Paris. Archaeological excavations have turned up traces of it.

Alfred the Great's reorganized *fyrd* (local militia) was able to sustain itself longer in the field, and his creation of a fleet of 60-oared vessels challenged the Vikings at sea and protected the coasts. Alfred also initiated the construction of a series of *burhs* or fortified settlements at regular intervals across Wessex. More than simply refuges in times of crisis, these were permanent planned settlements and centers of commerce that helped to check the movement of Scandinavian armies in southern England and served as a disincentive to settlement.

Nobles and ecclesiastical officials also took measures against the Northmen. Local nobles defended Aquitaine in the 830s, the Loire region in the 860s, Flanders in the 890s, and Brittany in the 930s, to take only a few examples. Kings did not necessarily always look favorably upon these actions, however, and Charles the Bald, for instance, was suspicious of the construction of fortifications by magnates. Bishops and abbots also led initiatives against Scandinavian invaders. The bishops of Orléans and Chartres successfully organized ships and soldiers against Vikings on the Loire in 854, and in 882 the bishop of Metz and the abbot of St-Martin of Tours independently raised armies against Vikings. Count Odo and Abbot Gauzlin heroically led the defense of Paris when it was besieged in 885–886.

We hear little about resistance by the lower orders of society, not because it did not occur, but because medieval sources were generally uninterested in peasants. Still, two episodes recorded in Frankish annals are illuminating. In 882, peasant tenants of the monastery of Prüm attempted an unsuccessful defense against Viking raiders, but were "slaughtered…like cattle." Earlier, when groups of peasants between the Seine and Loire rivers banded together against Viking raiders in 859, they were crushed—not by the Northmen, but by Frankish magnates, who feared a challenge to their own authority. As one scholar explains, "The Frankish élite might choose to defend their own social position in preference to their own people" (Nelson 1997, 44).

Since the Vikings were attracted by portable wealth, they could be bought off with tribute, often known as *danegeld* in England. Kings, local rulers, or ecclesiastical officials could organize such tributes. The Frankish king Charles the Bald offered a large fleet of Northmen on the Seine 7,000 lb of silver to spare Paris in 845, the first of many such tributes; it has been estimated (based on references in contemporary texts) that between 845 and 926 the Franks paid 685 lb of gold and 43,000 lb of silver in tribute to the Northmen. Much of this was acquired from church treasuries (and not always voluntarily given), but tributes were sometimes raised by royal taxation, as in 866 and 877 in the west Frankish kingdom. The Anglo-Saxon rulers of tenth- and early eleventh-century England also paid copious amounts of silver to buy off Viking raiders. Predictably, these payments attracted further raids that demanded larger and larger amounts of silver as tribute, rising from 10,000 lb in 991 to 21,000 lb in 1014; the English paid as much as 250,000 lb to the Vikings in 50 years.

The Vikings were not universally resisted, and in fact they were sometimes welcomed as useful allies in local political or dynastic struggles. In 838, following the arrival of a great Viking fleet in Cornwall, the Britons of Cornwall and the Northmen joined forces and fought against the West Saxons; the Vikings thereby became new players in a centuries-old conflict. On the Continent, the rulers of Brittany regularly hired Scandinavians for their own purposes, and the Vikings have been described as more help than hindrance to the Bretons in the late ninth century. In Ireland the Northmen were quickly integrated into Irish dynastic struggles, most famously perhaps at the battle of Clontarf in 1014. Once regarded as a national struggle by the Irish against the pagan Viking invaders, scholars now view Clontarf primarily as an Irish civil conflict in which Scandinavians fought on both sides.

Scandinavian warlords in the employ of European rulers make frequent appearances in contemporary texts. One of the most famous was Weland, a Viking leader on the Somme employed by Charles the Bald in the early 860s (see box 1.3). In England, the practice is attested in the late tenth and early eleventh centuries. As a logical extension of this phenomenon, European rulers sometimes granted territories to groups of Northmen in return for their assistance against other Viking groups. The grant of a territory at the mouth of the Seine to the Viking chieftain Hrolf (more commonly styled Rollo) ca 911 by the Frankish king Charles the Simple is not the earliest known instance of this practice, but it is the most significant and best known. Hrolf was made count of Rouen and so became—at least in theory—part of the Carolingian regime, and out of that grant the medieval duchy of Normandy was born.

One of the most famous responses to Viking settlement in England is the so-called Saint Brice's Day (13 November) massacre of 1002, when King Athelred II (r. 978–1016) ordered "all the Danes who had sprung up in this island, sprouting like weeds amongst the wheat...to be destroyed by a most just extermination" (Swanton 2000, 135 n.9). The episode is puzzling. Considerable numbers of Danes had been settled in northern England for well over a century by then, and the order never seems to have been carried out across all of England. Nevertheless, the Danes of Oxford, seeking sanctuary in Saint Frideswide's church, were burned inside by the local population. Explanations of the event by modern historians are diverse: some regard it as a specific and localized response, others as revenge for decades of Viking atrocities.

BOX 1.3 *Weland: Viking Warlord for Hire*

The career of Weland, a Scandinavian warlord who was active in the late 850s and early 860s, illustrates aspects of ninth-century Viking activity and European responses to it. The leader of a fleet on the Somme, Weland was hired by Charles the Bald in 860 to attack another group of Vikings, based on the island of Oissel in the Seine, in return for 3,000 lb of silver. When payment was delayed, Weland crossed the Channel and plundered in England, returning in 861. The Frankish king then agreed to pay Weland 5,000 lb of silver as well as livestock and supplies. Weland duly went off to fight the Seine Vikings, but when, forced by hunger and misery, they upped the stakes and offered even more tribute—6,000 lb of gold and silver—Weland changed sides and allied with them. Charles the Bald soon forced the troublesome Vikings to leave the kingdom, but Weland did not accompany them. Instead, along with his wife and sons he accepted Christianity and resided at the Frankish court as a "faithful man" of the king. In 863 he was killed in single combat after being accused of disloyalty to the king by some of his own men. Weland's career illustrates not only the existence of separate war-bands under their own leaders operating in the Frankish kingdoms, but also one of the preferred methods of Frankish rulers of dealing with these attacks by recruiting one group of Vikings to use against others.

Overall, Scandinavian raiders enjoyed the greatest success against politically decentralized regions such as Ireland and Scotland or the Frankish kingdoms after 843. Less success occurred when the Vikings came up against the sophisticated empires of Byzantium and Islam, or when kingdoms such as England became politically unified and able to resist more effectively. Not surprisingly, Viking success has sometimes been attributed to the weakness of their prey rather than to any inherent advantages the Vikings themselves possessed. This can be seen in the Viking ability to exploit the internal dissent that accompanied the break-up of the Carolingian empire from the 840s to the 880s.

BOX 1.4 *Archaeological Evidence for Viking Raiding*

Archaeological investigations have uncovered new evidence that contributes to our understanding of Viking raiding. At Portmahomack,

Tarbat, near Tain in northern Scotland, excavations of a Pictish monastery revealed evidence of burning, devastation, and human burials displaying evidence of sword marks, all dating from around 800. At Llanbedrgoch, on the island of Anglesey in north Wales, archaeologists examined a ninth-century settlement, where human skeletons had been unceremoniously dumped in a ditch; in one instance an adult male had been thrown directly on top of a child, and the adult seems to have had his hands tied behind his back. In the small Dutch town of Zutphen, excavations revealed a scene of early medieval carnage beneath the modern ground level: the burnt remains of timber buildings were found, and inside them were the skeletons of an adult and child, seemingly left unburied in the huts. Viking raiding activity is suspected as the cause of the carnage at all of these sites. One of the most striking new pieces of archaeological evidence for Viking raiding is the so-called Inchmarnock "hostage stone," which was discovered in two pieces during excavation of an early medieval chapel on the island of Inchmarnock, near Bute in the Clyde estuary of Scotland. The stone is a small, flat beach pebble. On one side a remarkable scene was scratched, showing a bearded male being led off to a ship by a long-haired warrior in chain mail; two other partial figures are also visible. Letters scratched on the reverse side date the find to the late eighth or early ninth century. It has been suggested that the stone may depict a Viking slave-raiding party, giving it unique status as a glimpse into Scandinavian raiding activities (Lowe 2007).

PHOTO 1.6   The Inchmarnock "Hostage Stone." (Photo courtesy of Chris Lowe)

"THE HEATHENS STAYED": THE SECOND VIKING AGE— CONQUEST AND SETTLEMENT

By the mid-ninth century, chroniclers in Ireland and England noted that Scandinavians were beginning to establish winter bases or camps in those regions, instead of retreating homewards at the end of the summer campaigning season. The development of overwintering followed a period of intensified raiding through the 830s. This marks a transitional phase between raiding and permanent settlement; overwintering on site meant more time to plunder. Some of the overwintering bases, such as Dublin, became permanent settlements, while others did not. Many scholars regard this phase of settlement as a "Second Viking Age" that was quite distinct from the "First Viking Age" and arguably more significant. This distinction is helpful, but it cannot be absolute; raiding contributed to Scandinavian knowledge of Britain and Europe and so helped pave the way for settlement. Moreover, settlement did not occur at the same time, or in the same manner, or to the same effect across Europe, and it is much better documented in some regions than in others.

The time lag between raiding and settlement varied regionally. In some places, the lag appears brief: settlement in Orkney and Shetland may have occurred as early as ca 800, although a date in the middle of the ninth century is favored. In Ireland, settlement followed an intensification of raiding through the 830s and was underway when a *longphort* or fortified naval base was constructed at Dubhlinn (Dublin) in 841; others followed, and some of them became urban centers. In England, settlement is associated with the activities of the so-called Great Army, which arrived from Denmark in 866 and wreaked havoc wherever it went, destroying the kingdoms of Northumbria, East Anglia, and Mercia between 866 and 870. An enigmatic entry in the *Anglo-Saxon Chronicle* for 878 relates how one of the army's leaders, Halfdan, "divided up the land of Northumbria; the raiders became tillers of the land as well." In the Isle of Man, the earliest evidence is archaeological and consists of a number of rich pagan burials of late ninth- and early tenth-century date. There is relatively little evidence for Viking settlement in Wales.

The most significant Scandinavian settlement on the Continent was in Normandy in the area around the mouth of the River Seine, downriver from Paris. Around 911 a Viking warlord named Hrolf received a grant of land along the Seine from the Frankish king Charles the Simple (d. 929); subsequent grants later extended the territory. Hrolf's Vikings were required to defend the territory from further attacks and to be baptized, showing how settlement led to assimilation. Further west, Brittany briefly endured what has been characterized as a military occupation from about 919 to 936, but the Vikings were eventually expelled.

A permanent Viking presence transformed existing political and social structures. In England, the rampages of the Great Army led to the elimination of major Anglo-Saxon kingdoms; only Wessex in the southwest survived, and even that was (particularly in the early 870s) a close-run thing. Investigations at Repton in England, where the Great Army overwintered in 873–874, have produced spectacular evidence of its destructive capacity. In North Britain, large areas of the western isles were wrested from Scottish control, becoming known to Gaelic speakers as *Innse Gall*, the Isles of the Foreigners. Parts of the northern mainland and the northern isles of Orkney and Shetland were removed from Pictish control, and the Picts themselves disappear from the written record in the late 870s. About the same time a new political entity, the kingdom of Alba, emerged, under the control of a dynasty descended from the mysterious Scottish warlord Cinaed son of Alpín (Kenneth MacAlpin, d. 858). There is no scholarly consensus on whether there was a Scandinavian contribution to this profound transformation of northern Britain. The Vikings made a less permanent impression on the political map of Ireland, where they failed to conquer on a similar scale to England or Scotland; apart from Dublin, Viking settlements were created in coastal locations at Waterford, Wexford, Cork, and Limerick, and a variety of forts and way-stations have also been identified. Since, however, many of these Scandinavian settlements in Ireland subsequently developed into urban centers, the Vikings may have had a significant economic impact.

BOX 1.5   *Repton, England: The Devastation of the Great Army*

Excavations at the Mercian royal monastery of Repton in Derbyshire, England, have produced impressive evidence of the destructive capacity of the Great Army, which, according to the *Anglo-Saxon Chronicle*, overwintered there in 873–874. When the church and churchyard were excavated in the 1980s, it was revealed that the Vikings had incorporated part of the existing church into a D-shaped rampart, showing no respect for the church or earlier burials. A number of burials were also excavated at the site. One was the grave of a warrior who had been mutilated post-mortem and was buried with a knife, a key, a sword that had been deliberately broken, a Thor's hammer amulet, and a boar's tusk and a jackdaw leg bone between his legs. He may have been one of the leaders of the Great Army. A Viking mass burial of some 264 individuals was found in an earlier Anglo-Saxon mausoleum outside the enclosure and may represent the remains of Viking warriors from the Great Army; it is thought they may have perished in an epidemic. The burial of four children nearby may be evidence of human sacrifice associated with the mass grave.

Settlement often led to the establishment of Scandinavian dynasties. In Ireland, the dynasty established by Olaf the White at Dublin in the 850s played an important role in the history of Ireland and the Irish Sea region for two centuries. In the wake of settlement, Irish Vikings were drawn into Irish politics, as Gaelic rulers hired them as allies in struggles with their rivals, demonstrating opportunism on both sides and shattering stereotypes of unity on either side. The battle of Clontarf (1014), long regarded as part of a "national" struggle by the Irish against the hated pagan Vikings, is now seen primarily as an Irish dynastic struggle in which Scandinavians were involved on both sides. In England, the leaders of the Great Army were styled kings and princes, and some of them settled down to rule at York (Jorvík), which became a flourishing urban center intermittently ruled by Viking kings until the death in 954 of Eirik Bloodax, a son of Harald Finehair (king of Norway, ca 880–930). Intermittent but important political and economic connections existed between Viking Dublin and York in the century between about 850 and 950. Irish Vikings settled Cumbria in northwestern England; the Cuerdale hoard, discovered in 1840 and comprising some 8,500 silver objects weighing nearly 88 lb, might represent the war chest of the Vikings of Dublin, who fled across the Irish Sea after their temporary expulsion from Dublin in 902.

Other parts of Britain also fell under the control of Scandinavian warlords such as Ketil Flatnose in the Hebrides (ca 840s-880) or the earls (*jarls*) of Orkney in Orkney and Shetland. The latter became major players in the politics of northern Britain, the Irish Sea, and the North Atlantic Viking world generally; their story forms the subject of *The Saga of the Orkney Islanders* (*Orkneyinga saga*). One of the most powerful of their number was Sigurd Hlodvisson "the Stout" (r. ca 985–1014), who fought and died in the battle of Clontarf in Ireland. Sigurd's presence at this conflict illustrates the international or transnational nature of the Viking world, since he fought as an ally of the Hiberno-Scandinavian king of Dublin, Sigtrygg Silkenbeard (r. 989–1036). In Normandy, the nature of the grant to Hrolf precluded a royal title, but his successors, the Norman counts (after 1006, dukes), became the most powerful of the French nobles in the eleventh century. They ruled a kingdom within a kingdom and cultivated their Scandinavian legacy while adopting French culture. Their most famous member was William "the Bastard" (1027–87), better known as "the Conqueror" after his conquest of England in 1066.

Determining the scale and impact of Viking settlement is problematic. The cryptic remark of the *Anglo-Saxon Chronicle* about the transition of some members of the Great Army from soldiers to colonists has already been noted. There is general agreement that the Scandinavian impact on England was substantial, but it is not certain whether this was the result of a relatively small group of warrior-elite settlers, of subsequent and undocumented mass migration, or of other processes. Scholarship on Viking settlement in Normandy favors the view that a relatively small Scandinavian elite ruled an existing Frankish population. Not surprisingly, assimilation seems to have followed, probably in an uneven and gradual manner that took about a century.

Another area where the nature of settlement is debated is the northern and western isles of Scotland. The fact of Viking settlement there is not in doubt, but unlike Ireland and England, where there is at least some documentary evidence for the process, there are no documentary sources at all, so linguistic and archaeological evidence assumes primary importance. Were the indigenous Picts of the northern isles enslaved, massacred, driven out, or assimilated by the Vikings? We don't really know, and scholarly debates on the subject are often heated. In the western isles of Scotland there was also Viking settlement, but it seems to have been less intense in nature than in Orkney and Shetland, and the density of settlement diminishes from north to south through the isles: there is denser settlement in Lewis and Skye than in Islay and Arran, for example. There is some evidence for intermarriage and interaction between incoming Vikings and existing Gaelic populations in the western isles, but little evidence for annihilation or eradication by Vikings; accordingly, cultural contact between Vikings, Picts, and Gaels constitutes an important theme in early Scottish and Scandinavian history. Similarly, on the Isle of Man the Norse do not seem to have completely displaced the existing population. The grave of a wealthy woman, excavated on Saint Patrick's island, Peel, in the 1980s (the so-called Pagan Lady of Peel), has been variously interpreted as that of the wife of an incoming Viking settler or, possibly, a native woman who adopted Scandinavian modes of dress and burial. A unique body of sculptural material, the Manx crosses, blend Irish and Scandinavian motifs and designs, and some of them contain runic inscriptions with both Irish and Scandinavian names, further suggesting a blending of cultures rather than the complete displacement of the natives.

Scandinavian settlement in Britain, Ireland, and Europe took many forms. In the northern and western isles of Scotland, settlement comprised individual farms and was entirely rural in nature: recent surveys on the most northerly of the Shetland Islands, Unst, have identified many Viking Age longhouse sites, individual and isolated farmsteads of Viking settlers. In Ireland, urban centers such as those at Dublin, Waterford, Limerick, and Wexford have dominated discussion of Viking settlement types. Archaeological excavations in Dublin since the 1960s have provided extensive evidence for tenth-century Scandinavian settlement, including dwellings, workshops, quays, and cemeteries; it is not an exaggeration to say that the Vikings introduced urban centers into predominantly rural Irish society. Recent scholarship, however, emphasizes a diversity of settlement types in Ireland, including towns but also highlighting military structures such as *longphorts* and other fortifications, as well as farmsteads and maritime way-stations. England, like Ireland, provides evidence of the varied nature of Scandinavian settlements. For example, excavations at York (Viking Jorvík) provide important evidence of commerce, commercial contacts, crafts, and trades in the Viking Age. On the other hand, Viking farmsteads in England have proven elusive, partly because they can be difficult to distinguish from Anglo-Saxon settlement types.

THE VIKING ROAD TO THE EAST

As raiding and settlement progressed in western Europe, Scandinavian merchants and mercenaries penetrated eastern Europe, where they came into contact with two great medieval powers, Byzantium and the Islamic world. This eastern expansion was largely the work of Swedes. Two terms, *Rūs* and *Væringjar* (Varangian), are used in western and eastern sources to describe the Swedish Vikings in the east. The derivation of the term *Rūs* is controversial and ultimately uncertain, but it may be derived from the Finnish name for the Swedes, *Ruotsi*, which itself is probably derived from an Old Swedish word meaning something like "rowers" or "seamen." The Rūs gave their name to Russia, although scholars have contested the extent to which they influenced Russian state formation. From the mid-tenth century the term "Varangian" also came into use. It may be derived from the Old Norse *vár* (pledge), and may refer to the groups of merchant-adventurers who bound themselves into companies and swore to support each other. The term was also used for foreign mercenaries and does not seem to have had specific ethnic associations.

From about the second half of the eighth century, Scandinavians were living at the trading center at Staraya (Old) Ladoga (known as *Aldeigjuborg* by the Scandinavians), just off Lake Ladoga on the River Volkhov. From this commanding position on the river routes, further eastward expansion followed. Drawn by the lure of Islamic silver, which was reaching Russia by the late eighth century, Scandinavian merchant-adventurers had discovered by the 830s how to travel south through Russia using the great river routes of eastern Europe: the Lovat (to Lake Ladoga and the Gulf of Finland), Dvina (to the Gulf of Riga and the Baltic), Dnieper (to the Black Sea), and Volga (to the Caspian). With the exception of places where ships had to be portaged to avoid rapids or to get from the headland of one river to another, it was possible to sail Viking ships from the Baltic to the Caspian Sea. This was the *austrvegr*, the way to the east, or the "Viking road to Byzantium" as it has famously been called, detailed knowledge of which is derived from Byzantine and Russian sources; a treatise written by the Byzantine emperor Constantine VII Porphyrogenitus (r. 945–959) preserves important information about the routes used by the voyagers to the east. Through these waterways, the Vikings eventually came into contact with both Byzantine and Islamic civilizations, encountering Slavs, Bulgars, Khazars, and other peoples along the way. Trade was the driving force of this eastward expansion, and some trade treaties of the Rūs with Byzantium are preserved in later medieval chronicles. Viking merchants traded furs, honey, wax, walrus ivory, high-grade weapons, and slaves, obtaining in return Arab silver—thousands of coins (*dirhams*) have been found in Scandinavian hoards, with many thousands more coming from Russian hoards.

Not all Viking voyages to the east were peaceful, and commerce was often inseparable from fighting. In 860 and 907, two unsuccessful attacks were mounted against the capital of the Eastern Roman Empire, Constantinople (Byzantium; modern Istanbul in Turkey), known to the Scandinavians as *Mikligarðr* ("the great city"). The attack of 907 was followed by trade treaties in 907 and 911. There was also sporadic raiding on the Caspian Sea into the middle of the eleventh century. Ultimately, however, both Islam and Byzantium, with their centralized governments and sophisticated military organizations, proved too tough for the Vikings to crack. Both Muslims and Byzantines recognized the warrior qualities of the Scandinavians. Islamic writers who commented on the Scandinavians in the east remarked on their martial abilities, and the Muslims prized Viking weapons, especially swords. Scandinavian mercenaries entered into military service with the Byzantine army, forming the emperor's bodyguard from the late tenth century. This elite "Varangian guard" was a stepping-stone in many Viking careers, including that of Harald Sigurdarson Hardradi before he became king of Norway (r. 1047–66); the sagas abound in Scandinavians who earned fame and fortune in the east before returning home. By about the middle of the ninth century, Scandinavians had also founded merchant towns such as Novgorod and taken control of existing settlements such as Kiev, and by the end of the century a state based on Novgorod and Kiev had emerged. Although the relationship between Scandinavians and Slavs in these regions is controversial, it seems likely that Scandinavian merchant-adventurers formed a ruling elite that eventually assimilated with the Slavic population.

INTO THE WESTERN OCEAN: THE NORTH ATLANTIC SAGA

Viking voyages to the northern and western isles in the early ninth century led indirectly to the discovery of islands further west in the North Atlantic, as mariners were blown off course and sighted new lands beyond their original destinations. It is possible that Viking contact with Irish monks in places such as Ireland and the Hebrides provided knowledge about islands such as the Faeroes and Iceland. Several early medieval writers, including the Irish monk Dicuil ca 825, indicate that Irish hermits had voyaged to the Faeroes and Iceland as part of the practice of *peregrinatio*, or voluntary exile. It has also been established that many of the early settlers in Iceland did not come directly from Norway but by way of the Hebrides, Ireland, or Scotland; some of them brought Gaelic slaves, concubines, or wives, and there was a substantial Gaelic contribution to Viking Age Iceland. Studies of the genetic makeup of modern Icelanders have revealed much about the origins of the early settlers.

Unlike the earliest phases of Viking activity in Britain and on the Continent, the North Atlantic saga was characterized from the beginning by settlement rather than raiding. With the exception of some Irish hermits, the North Atlantic islands were uninhabited, so there were no local populations to raid and no opposition to overcome in order to take lands. Although the Faeroes, Iceland, and Greenland may appear bleak and uninviting to modern travelers, they had much to offer Viking colonists. With their deeply indented fjords, sheltered dales, cliffs, and mountains, these lands were geographically similar to Norway, and Norwegian emigrants would have felt at home here (most of the settlers in the North Atlantic came from Norway). Although generally not well suited to the growing of crops, these lands were very suitable for the pasturing of animals, which was more important to the pastoral agriculture practiced by most of the Scandinavians. Still another attraction was the abundance of resources provided by the proximity to the ocean. Exploitation of walrus may have preceded large-scale settlement in Iceland and Greenland and may even have led the Norse Greenlanders into trade relations with the Dorset and Thule cultures of the eastern Canadian Arctic.

The discovery of new lands in the western ocean was characterized by a pattern of accidental discovery followed (sometimes much later) by exploration and settlement. Storm-driven Scandinavians en route to the Faeroes first sighted Iceland; these discoveries cannot be dated precisely, but the twelfth-century historical text *Íslendingabók* (*The Book of Icelanders*) puts the earliest settlement there at 870. Archaeology bears out such a date: excavations in the center of Reykjavík in 2001 revealed the remains of a longhouse datable to the year 871 (+/− 2), and the site has been turned into the superb Landnámssýningin or Settlement Exhibition. Like Iceland, Greenland was first sighted by sailors blown off course: Gunnbjorn Ulf-Krakason spotted new lands to the west of Iceland when he was driven across the ocean by a storm, but it was left to the famous Norwegian Eirik Thorvaldsson, better known as Eirik the Red, to explore and colonize the land Gunnbjorn had discovered (see chapter 3). Gunnbjorn's voyage cannot be dated with certainty: it perhaps took place around 900, while Eirik's reconnaissance and colonization occurred in the early and mid-980s. Eirik's son Leif ("the Lucky") retraced the steps of the storm-driven Bjarni Herjolfsson to unknown lands west of Greenland: Helluland ("Slab-rock Land," probably Baffin Island), Markland ("Forest Land," probably Labrador), and Vínland ("Wine Land," now thought to be the Gulf of St. Lawrence region).

Land hunger may have been one motivation for the colonization of the North Atlantic islands, but according to Icelandic tradition there was also a political dimension. Many of the sagas relate that the early settlers of the Faeroes and Iceland were chieftains fleeing the tyrannical rule of King Harald Finehair of Norway following the battle of Hafsfjord. Modern scholarship is skeptical of this claim, however, since the settlement of Iceland began in the early 870s, perhaps as much as two decades before the battle of Hafsfjord is believed to have occurred (ca 885–890). Still, since this motif occurs in so many of the sagas, and since many of the early settlers were important Norwegian chieftains, it is possible that the beginnings of the consolidation of power of the Norwegian monarchy did play some role in the expansion into the western ocean.

Viking contact with North America appears to have been a brief affair. Archaeological evidence from the site at L'Anse aux Meadows in Newfoundland seems to indicate that it was used for only a few decades at the start of the eleventh century. L'Anse aux Meadows is possibly the *Leifsbúðir* and/or *Straumsfjörðr* of the *Vínland sagas* (*Eirik the Red's Saga* and *Saga of the Greenlanders*). A substantial body of Norse material has been recovered from Dorset and Thule sites in the eastern Canadian Arctic that seems to tell a story of sustained trade and cultural interactions over several centuries—although the interpretation of this material remains contentious. Whatever the case may be, the Norse presence in North America represented both the westernmost limit of Viking expansion and the first coming together of the European and American continents. The Norse colonies in Greenland endured for some five centuries after their founding in the 980s; the reasons for their demise in the fourteenth and fifteenth centuries still generate controversy.

MERCHANTS AND MERCENARIES

Emphasis on the dramatic processes of raiding, conquest, and settlement may overshadow other forms of interaction. Much contact was commercial in nature. Commercial connections may have made the Scandinavians aware of the relative wealth of western Europe, Britain, and Ireland in the first place. Scandinavian merchants ranged from Newfoundland to Constantinople and into the Islamic world, and trade flowed through market centers at Hedeby in Denmark, Visby and Birka in Sweden, Kaupang in Norway, Dublin in Ireland, York in England, Novgorod in Russia, and Kiev in the Ukraine. Scandinavian merchants traded with the Franks, and Frankish missionaries traveled to Scandinavia in company with merchants. The Norwegian chieftain Ohthere presented King Alfred of Wessex with a gift of walrus ivory. In the thirteenth-century Norwegian text *The King's Mirror*, a father offers his son far-ranging advice on mercantile activities. Archaeology enhances this picture. Thousands of Islamic silver coins (*dirhams*) are known from archaeological sites in Viking Age Scandinavia, glittering testimony to lucrative relations between Scandinavian merchants and their Islamic counterparts, for these are thought to represent the fruits of trade rather than raiding. A fragment of a bronze scale recovered from a Thule Inuit site on Ellesmere Island in northern Canada may have belonged to a Norse merchant and points to formal trade with the Thule people that is undocumented in written sources. A necklace recovered from the grave of a woman in the Isle of Man was made of beads gathered from all over the Viking world. Exotic items recovered from Viking Age occupation levels in York, England, included silk and a cowrie shell native to the Persian Gulf, testimony to long-range commercial contacts between the Viking world and the Near and Middle East.

Trading and raiding could also be two sides of the same coin, and commerce as well as raiding offered a path to fame and fortune. The occupation of a Viking, in the original sense of the term, was after all a part-time one, so the same individual could be both raider and trader—sometimes even engaging in both activities on the same expedition. *Egil's Saga*, for example, one of the finest of the Icelandic family sagas (see chapter 4), preserves a wealth of information on Scandinavian society, although it cannot be taken as a straightforward historical source. The saga describes how, on one occasion, its hero, Egil Skallagrimsson, and his brother Thorolf, "...raided in the east where they fought a good many battles and acquired a great deal of plunder. Then they made for Courland where they moored offshore and traded peacefully for a couple of weeks. But when they were done with trading, they started raiding again, going ashore at a number of different places."

Serving as mercenaries was another means for Scandinavians to acquire fame and fortune. The example of the Varangian guard of Byzantium has already been noted, but this was not the only instance of Scandinavians serving in the armies of European powers. At one time or another during the Viking Age, Scandinavian warriors could be found fighting for most European kingdoms and rulers, against both other European rulers and other groups of

Scandinavians. Frankish annals and chronicles reveal that many Scandinavian warlords found themselves in the service of ninth-century Frankish kings. British and Irish sources show how Vikings were drawn into struggles between different Irish kingdoms or between British and Anglo-Saxon kingdoms. In *Egil's Saga*, the protagonist, Egil, and his brother, Thorolf, sought out and served the English king Athelstan as mercenaries at the battle of Brunanburh (937). As the Vikings became involved in such disputes, battle-lines grew blurred, as was the case in the battle of Clontarf.

THE END OF THE VIKING AGE

When and how did the Viking Age end? The beginning of the era is marked by the onset of raiding at the end of the eighth century, but the close of the Viking Age is less well defined, perhaps because, in contrast to the beginning of the Viking Age, it has been largely neglected by scholars. Traditionally, a variety of markers have been used. These include the conversion of the Scandinavians to Christianity, which brought them into the mainstream of the religious culture of western Europe; the development of unitary Christian kingships in Scandinavia, which brought the kingdoms of the region into line with other European kingdoms; and military events such as the defeat of King Harald Hardradi Sigurdarson of Norway at the Battle of Stamford Bridge in September 1066, often cited as the last large-scale Viking expedition (see chapter 3). Curiously, the cessation of raiding is a criterion that is seldom examined in evaluating the end of the Viking Age. But even this is difficult to assess, as small-scale raiding parties of the late eighth and early ninth centuries gave way to larger, better-organized armies and fleets in the ninth century, and later still to royal expeditions intent on the political takeover of England in the late tenth and early eleventh centuries.

History seldom provides neat delineations between arbitrary "ages" imposed by historians, and because of the wide extent of the Scandinavian diaspora it is impossible to identify a single date that has meaning throughout the Viking world. As we have seen, the Viking Age itself was not a monolithic chronological period spanning some three or four centuries but was marked by a variety of distinct phases of activity and by both continuity and change. Thus, the conversion to Christianity was not a single momentous event but rather a continuum that spanned almost the entire Viking Age. Or, to take another perspective, Scandinavian influence in the Scottish islands lasted until the second half of the thirteenth century, long after it had waned in England, Ireland, or Normandy. In the North Atlantic, Iceland and Greenland remained independent of Norway until late in the reign of King Hakon IV (r. 1217–63), when they were finally brought under Norwegian suzerainty, ending 400 and 300 years respectively of autonomy from Norway. A quest for military milestones is equally subject to regional constraints. While the defeat of the Norwegian king Harald Hardradi Sigurdarson at the Battle of Stamford Bridge in September 1066 is commonly taken to mark the end of the period in England, the date has little relevance in other parts of the British Isles. In an Irish Sea context, the great expedition of Magnus "Barelegs," another king of Norway, in 1098 offers an equally impressive candidate for the swansong of the era; no Scandinavian king appeared again in the waters off Britain until Hakon IV of Norway's ill-fated expedition in the autumn of 1263. In an eastern context, the famous expedition of Ingvar ca 1040 merits inclusion. Consideration of culture rather than politics may yield very different answers to the question of when the Viking Age ended. Skaldic poetry, for example, spans the period from the ninth to the fourteenth century, and its chronological limit is usually considered to be around 1400, but after the introduction of Christianity, Christian themes gradually replaced the pre-Christian themes of the earlier period. In the end, then, it is probably impossible to define the end of the Viking Age, and we must be content with acknowledging that it drew to a close at different times depending on the region under consideration, or the criteria used.

THE VIKINGS IN THE COURTROOM OF HISTORY: TERRORISTS, TOURISTS, OTHERS

The Vikings have long been accused in the courtroom of history of being nothing more than ax-wielding barbarians who raped, pillaged, and plundered their way across Europe in the early Middle Ages, with dire consequences for Western civilization, which, so the story goes, scraped through only by the skin of its teeth, as Kenneth Clark memorably put it in his epic and now rather old-fashioned book on Western civilization (Clark 1969). Indeed, the Vikings have been blamed for everything from a decline in learning, thanks to the destruction of churches and monasteries, the centers of learning in the early Middle Ages, to the break-up of the Carolingian empire in the ninth century. But has history been fair to the Vikings?

In 1962 the historian Peter Sawyer began a revolution in traditional views of the Vikings. In *The Age of the Vikings*, Sawyer argued that the Vikings were the victims of a bad press at the hands of medieval Christian chroniclers, who exaggerated the size of Viking fleets and armies and the violence that they perpetrated. Setting aside exaggerations in the sources, Sawyer claimed that Viking raids were unexceptional in the broader early medieval context: "Once the prejudices and exaggerations of the primary sources are recognized, the raids can be seen not as an unprecedented and inexplicable cataclysm, but as an extension of normal Dark Age activity, made possible and profitable by special circumstances" (Sawyer 1962, 194).

Sawyer's thesis found widespread support in the 1960s and 1970s. Excavations from Viking Age levels of settlements such as Dublin and York bolstered the image of the Vikings as peaceful merchants, traders, and settlers. By 1970 the "Viking achievement" (Foote and Wilson 1970) stood shoulder to shoulder with the "glory that was Greece" and the "grandeur that was Rome" in a popular series of books dealing with great civilizations. The Vikings had, in little more than a decade, been transformed from illiterate and barbaric destroyers to the creators of a distinct civilization. One critic summarized the new image of the Vikings by observing that they had become little more than "groups of long-haired tourists who occasionally roughed up the natives" (Wallace-Hadrill 1976, 220).

Even tourists can be destructive, however, and the "new Vikings" of the 1960s and 1970s did not satisfy everyone. By the 1990s the so-called revisionist school was under fire, as scholars such as Alfred P. Smyth (1999) and David Dumville (1997) cast doubt on Sawyer's arguments and re-opened debates about the Vikings' destructive capacity. These scholars returned to a view that emphasized the Viking penchant for brutal and violent behavior and the terror it instilled, even if it was perpetrated only by relatively small groups: "Conclusions reached by revisionists on the Viking Age do not stand up to scrutiny . . . we are faced with a catalogue of atrocities carried out by an invading people who did not share the belief systems of their victims" (Smyth 1999, 33).

A key component of this argument turns on the paganism of the Vikings: not only could the Scandinavians, as non-Christians, not be expected to play by the same set of rules as their Christian neighbors and victims, but Smyth has also argued that "Norse culture—and therefore Norse paganism—lent a particularly vicious edge to Norse raiding" (1999, 27). The Vikings thus return to being "illiterate barbarians" (the term is Smyth's) who could only destroy European civilization; in the course of rebutting the views of the revisionist school, Smyth and others have created a new view of the Vikings that treats them as even more horrible than they had been reckoned before.

It is thus possible to construct the Vikings as "Others," and more specifically as non-Christian Others who did not share the values of the rest of western Europe and therefore did not play by the same rules. The language used to describe the raiders in ninth-century texts, where they are not typically defined in racial or ethnic terms but rather are most commonly described as "heathens" or "pagans," can be cited as evidence in support of this view. Yet, while treating the Vikings in this manner has undoubtedly advanced our understanding of Viking activities, it may nevertheless prove possible to overestimate the extent to which they were different.

Were they, for example, any more violent than their Christian neighbors, victims, and rivals? For scholars who have examined the problem, the answer is that raiding, plundering, tribute-taking, and cruelty to rivals were defining characteristics of early medieval warfare and were by no means monopolized by the Vikings: "Few people lived in security from hostile plundering raids in the post-Roman west" (Halsall 1992, 4; see also Reuter 1985; Lund 1989). Scholars point to atrocities perpetrated by the Franks and Anglo-Saxons upon their enemies, rivals, and captured opponents (Halsall 1992, 3; Earl 1999, 126). It has further been observed that many aspects of Viking warfare seem to have differed little from those of the Franks or Anglo-Saxons: "Scarcely a year went by in the Frankish kingdoms without some kind of military activity, either between the Frankish realms themselves, or against their neighbors" (Halsall 1992, 4). Einhard, the biographer of the Frankish king Charlemagne, preserves in his work the medieval saying "Have a Frank as a friend, never as a neighbor."

Other studies have suggested that violence against churches and monasteries may also have been more prevalent in early medieval society than was once thought (Foot 1991, 5–6); one scholar has remarked bluntly that "the Vikings were not the only church robbers in Francia any more than they were in Ireland" (Reuter 1985, 78). Viking paganism may have taken disrespect of Christian holy places to new levels, however, as well as encouraging further Christian violence against churches (Lucas 1967; Halsall 1992). In many respects, then, the Vikings were little different from their neighbors in the British Isles and on the Continent, something that is suggested by the willingness of European, British, and Irish rulers to employ Vikings in their own political struggles. Perhaps, as one scholar suggests, "what upset Europe probably was most of all that these newcomers to the game had such success and managed to reverse the flow of money, embarrassing traditional tribute-takers by making them tribute-payers" (Lund 1989, 45).

Similarly, the story of Scandinavian–European contacts suggests that Viking Otherness was insufficient to prevent interactions on a variety of levels. Significant diplomatic and political contacts existed between the Danes and the Frankish rulers of the Carolingian kingdoms, for instance, and then there is the case of the Norwegian chieftain Ohthere, who visited the English king Alfred sometime during his reign (871–899); was he perhaps a guest at court and not just a visiting merchant (Lund 1984, 13)? We may note also instances of cooperation between Scandinavian merchants and Frankish missionaries in the early ninth century. One conclusion that can be drawn from these examples is that the Vikings can hardly have been as alien as they are sometimes made out to be.

One lesson from all of this is that scholarship is continually changing and developing. Another lesson is that the issues are incredibly complex and multifaceted. Simplistic views of the Vikings as either terrorists or tourists overlook key aspects of Scandinavian behavior and attempt to force the Vikings into rigid molds. Scandinavians could be both raiders and traders on the same expedition, as circumstances dictated. Similarly, while there is much to be said for viewing the Vikings as "A Different Thing" (Halsall 1992, 2), this, too, seems to ignore the many and varied interactions that Scandinavians enjoyed with their neighbors, rivals, and victims. Put another way, the Vikings were clearly not so different that no one wanted to do business with them: recall, for instance, the many Scandinavian warlords such as Weland hired by Frankish kings in the ninth century. Still another problem is that debate has tended, perhaps unsurprisingly, to concentrate upon raiding and violence to the exclusion of much else. Take, for instance, the Viking Egil Skallagrimsson (ca 910–990): though a brutal killer and hardened warrior, Egil was a master of poetry who composed a powerful poem on the death of his sons (see chapters 3 and 4) and was also something of a lawyer. Given such complexities, the debate is unlikely to be resolved anytime soon.

Two further points suggest themselves. First, historical writing does not occur in a vacuum, and historical interpretations often tell us as much about the period in which they were written as about the period under scrutiny. Every generation, it has been said, writes its own history. It may therefore be no coincidence that Sawyer's thesis emerged in a post-war Europe that not only still exhibited the scars of the World War II, but had also seen the Vikings used in various ways by the National Socialists. To take but one example, the name given to one of the elite panzer divisions of the Waffen SS, composed largely of volunteers from the Scandinavian countries, was *Wiking* (*Viking*). Does Sawyer's view of the Vikings owe anything to this background? Was post-war Europe fertile ground for kinder, gentler Vikings? Similarly, is it significant that Smyth's and Dumville's interpretations of the Vikings took shape at the end of the twentieth century, when the horrors of war, genocide, famine, and terrorism once more dominated the headlines? Do different views of the Vikings, then, reflect, at least in part, the environments in which they have been produced?

Finally, what is perhaps most remarkable about the nature of scholarship on the Vikings since the 1960s is that most of these different and sometimes opposing views are derived from the same body of evidence: principally, but not solely, contemporary British, Irish, and European chronicles, annals, and other written accounts. What actually leads to the plethora of differing views of the Vikings is the manner in which scholars utilize this evidence. Thus, one broader historical principle highlighted by the debate relates to the fundamental role of interpretation in scholarship. As one scholar succinctly put it, "That sources on which so much depends are so open to interpretation and reinterpretation is what makes the study of the Viking period so fascinating" (Lund 1989, 59). Here, at least, it is difficult to disagree.

CHAPTER TWO

SOCIETY AND RELIGION IN THE VIKING AGE

RANK

The eddic poem known as *The Lay of Rig* (*Rígsþula*) divides mankind into three social orders. The poem accompanies the god Heimdall, under the name of Rig, on his visits to three couples with whom he has relations: great-grandmother and great-grandfather; grandmother and grandfather; father and mother. After the god's visit, the three couples produce children: Thrall (slave), Karl (freeman), and Jarl (earl). These represent a tripartite division of the social order in which Thrall alone is unfree. Karl is a free farmer and Jarl has political and military responsibilities. The poem is incomplete and there is uncertainty about the ending, in which Rig appears to be preparing a son of Jarl to become king. Although the poem probably presents a simplistic view of Scandinavian social organization, it does reveal a social ideology, as well as the work associated with the different orders.

Norse society was more complex and less static than *The Lay of Rig* suggests. The earliest kings in Scandinavia were probably regional warlords whose position rested more on their ability and the support of their followers than on inheritance. Earlier kings also had to pay attention to the decisions of regional assemblies (*thing*: ON *þing*) made up of local freemen and gentry. In the tenth century, kings who aspired to be rulers of the whole of Norway increasingly rested their claims to the throne on their sometimes tenuous descent from Harald Finehair (ca 850–ca 933). With the coming of Christianity, the idea of the king as God's anointed gradually took hold. This idea was firmly established in Norway during the reign of Hakon IV Hakonarson (1204–63), who went to considerable lengths to have himself crowned by the pope's representative. He arranged, too, for the coronation of his son, Magnus, in his own lifetime.

Hakon IV's reign exemplified other trends at work in Scandinavian kingship. Hakon was no longer a Viking chieftain or warlord who enforced his rule through his control of a *hirð* (military elite). Hakon ruled a centralized state with an organization that resembled a civil service. This movement toward centralization and civil government began throughout Scandinavia in the tenth century, developing more rapidly in Denmark than elsewhere. The transformation of Scandinavian warlords into national, hereditary monarchs is closely related to the arrival of Christianity in the region. The church provided a model for centralized government and offered kings a sacral legitimacy, expressed in ceremonies such as coronation. With Christianity, European notions of the state and government entered Scandinavia. By the time of Hakon IV, regional assemblies had little more than a token function, although Hakon still thought it worthwhile to have himself recognized as king by them.

The aristocracy is represented only by Jarl in *The Lay of Rig*, but the reality was considerably more varied. *Jarls* were originally landed warlords, not unlike the early kings themselves. Their titles were frequently heritable, and the independence of *jarls*, such as the *jarl* of Lade in Norway, was a threat to royal power. It was not until the eleventh century that Norwegian kings succeeded in reining in the power of the *jarls*. Another title associated with the ruling classes was *lendr maðr* (landed man). *Lendr maðr*, however, was not a hereditary title, but a royal appointment with specific responsibilities. The position was often given to members of aristocratic or prominent families.

Below kings and aristocrats were freemen. A fundamental distinction among the free depended on land tenure. Those who inherited rights to land over several generations (odal rights) were distinguished from others who merely rented or bought land. In Norway, possessors of odal rights were known as *höldr* and formed a yeomanry with a strong sense of its rights and independence. The foundation narratives of several Icelandic sagas (for instance, *The Saga of the People of Laxardale, Egil's Saga*) describe the resentment of hereditary landowners required to surrender their odal rights to Harald Finehair. Below the *höldr* came the *bóndi* (pl. *bœndr*). The term *bóndi* included any free farmer, however humble his holding.

SLAVERY

Although slavery was important in the Viking Age, its extent and duration are both uncertain. The slave trade was a significant part of raiding and trading in the west. Some merchants may have dealt only in slaves, but many probably had a diversified trade. Slaves were drawn from all areas subjected to Viking raids. In the saga-literature, Irish slave names are frequent. Although African captives are mentioned, slaves were generally European. In the east, there is evidence of an extensive slave trade carried on by the Rūs along the Russian river-systems. Most slaves in Scandinavia and Iceland were probably domestic slaves, sharing in the regular work of farming households. Their tasks were in the main no different from the work of most of the free people around them. Like women, slaves were exempted from the duties and excluded from the rights of what we might call citizenship.

The Book of Settlements (*Landnámabók*) suggests that early settlers in Iceland brought as many as 10 slaves per household, though one Scandinavian law code implies that a modest farmer's household might be expected to have no more than three slaves. In eleventh-century Norway, Erling Skjalgsson had a household of 80 retainers and 30 slaves, all of whom were expected to buy their freedom, implying that he could rely on a continuing supply of new slaves. Erling, however, was a powerful man and a great landowner.

Slaves were the legal property of their owners and had no personal *réttr* (rights, worth). In cases where payment was made for the death or injury of a slave, the compensation was for damage to the owner's property and related to the cost of the slave, rather than to any personal rights or worth. Nonetheless, slaves sometimes had the legal right to a share in the compensation; in Iceland this was usually a third of the amount paid. Law and literature both imply that slaves might possess property, but it is not clear that they had any right to defend it. While law codes offer some recognition of slave marriages, slave families are hardly mentioned in law or in the sagas. The rights of slave parents over their children must have been severely limited by the hereditary nature of slave status. Slaves might purchase or be granted freedom, but the taint of servility often survived since freedmen (*leysingi*) and their children generally still owed certain obligations to their erstwhile owners for several generations.

The social status of slaves is uncertain. *Rígsþula*, for example, contrasts light-skinned, handsome freemen with dark and ugly thralls. However, scholarly opinion is divided about the interpretation of *Rígsþula*. In the *Saga of Geirmundr Heljarskin*, the true nobility of the aristocrat shines through his swarthy countenance. Elsewhere in the saga-literature, slaves can be strong, manly types, though one of the earliest episodes recounted in *Landnámabók* is the betrayal and murder of Herjolfr by his Irish slaves.

The sagas of Icelanders suggest that slavery died out in Iceland in the early tenth century. In Norway, late thirteenth-century law codes fail to mention slavery. Elsewhere in Scandinavia, the late thirteenth and fourteenth centuries probably saw the end of the institution. The cause of this decline is not clear. It may be that the supply of affordable slaves dried up after the Viking Age, but that cannot explain why slaves as a class died out. Some historians suggest that the rarity of large-scale demesne farming in Scandinavia made slavery unnecessary. Another way of seeing this is that expansion of tenant farming made the possession of slave workforces unnecessary. Landowners probably found it cheaper to have tenants who looked after their own needs rather than slaves whose upkeep was the landowner's responsibility. It may be, simply, that as tenant farming increased, the distinction between landowner and tenant became socially and economically dominant, and people came to see themselves as either owning land or leasing it.

WOMEN

The Lay of Rig confines women to domestic roles. The slave's wife might work in the fields, but the karl's wife was engaged in spinning and weaving. Again, the reality was more complex. The evidence of Viking Age graves, for instance, suggests that women also engaged in commerce. In *The Saga of the Greenlanders*, Freydis, daughter of Eirik the Red, leads a voyage to Vínland, where she distinguishes herself by her bloody-minded competitiveness.

Women had the right to own, inherit, and manage property. One of the principal early settlers of Iceland was Unn the Deep-Minded (fl. ca 900; see chapter 3). She claimed a huge land take and, like any other important settler, distributed land among her followers. She freed slaves and, unusually, arranged marriages for men. The case of Unn is a reminder that Norse expansion involved considerable numbers of women from a wide range of backgrounds. Though Norse women appear not to have accompanied their men on raiding trips, finds of Scandinavian women's jewelry suggest the presence of Norse women in the Danelaw (the area of Danish settlement in England). Scandinavian graves in Scotland also provide evidence of women who were Norse in origin. It should not be forgotten that Unn herself traveled to Iceland after a long residence in Scotland.

Women enjoyed an ambiguous socio-political status in the Viking Age. Though they were subject to the law and its penalties, women had no right to defend themselves in court. A woman with legal difficulties had to find a male advocate. While a woman could inherit the position of *goði* (pl. *goðar*: often anglicized as *godi*: an Icelandic local chieftain), her status forbade her from performing its duties. She could not sit down with other *goðar* at the

Althing (*Alþing*, the Icelandic national assembly) to conduct the political and legal business (for example, sitting on juries) that was largely the point of the meeting. Women hover on the margins of these assemblies. This disability had the advantage of removing women from the serious physical violence that frequently accompanied legal disputes, both at and away from the *thing*.

The Christianization of the north is sometimes regarded as having deprived women of earlier liberties. This may be partly true. In the case of marriage, for example, the Church did teach that women's consent was required. In theory, this removed some of the power of male relatives over women. But, strange to say, the sagas of Icelanders recount several instances where a pre-Christian woman was consulted about her betrothal, whereas such consultation is remarkably absent from thirteenth-century contemporary sagas that recount events that took place long after Christianization.

As for divorce, the Christian Church forbade it, though the ruling was not always enforced. In pre-Christian times, however, both the sagas and the laws gave both men and women the right to divorce. Women retained ownership of their dowries and had the right to keep them as well as the bride-price in a divorce. Sagas suggest that a further division of the marital property could also be made. This state of affairs is understandable in a society in which betrothal was originally a contract sealed with a handshake, rather than a promise made before God. As the case of Vigdis and Thord Goddi (*The Saga of the People of Laxardale*) shows, a woman had often to rely on the support of her birth-family to ensure a fair division of the property. Here (and in *Gisli's Saga*) it is clear that married women retained a strong connection with their birth-families. The strength of this connection is exemplified in the heroic poem *The Lay of Atli* (*Atlakviða*), where Gudrun does not hesitate to destroy her husband and their children to avenge her dead brothers.

Norse literature suggests that women were able to exert influence in a variety of extra-legal ways. The women of *The Saga of the People of Laxardale*, for instance, are an astonishingly strong group. Unn the Deep-Minded has already been mentioned, but she was not alone in her assertiveness. Thorgerd, daughter of Egil Skallagrimsson, insists on being consulted about her marriage with Olaf the Peacock Hoskuldsson, though Egil has the legal right to dispose of her as he wishes. Later in the same saga, Thorgerd shames her sons into taking revenge for her murdered son, Kjartan Olafsson. Another assertive woman is Vigdis, wife of Thord Goddi, who exhibits strong, decisive behavior that contrasts sharply with her husband's lack of manliness, and in the latter part of the saga, Gudrun Osvifrsdaughter exerts a powerful if not entirely benign influence. Like many other strong women in the sagas, her influence depends on her ability to persuade or shame men into taking public action on her behalf.

The Saga of the People of Laxardale is not a historical document, however, and it is far from certain that the saga preserves authentic memories of the women of the tenth century. Nonetheless, together with heroic poems such as *Atlakviða*, the sagas of Icelanders present a complex ideology of women's behavior and duties.

FAMILIES

The nuclear family was the household norm in the Viking Age. The typical Viking Age boat-shaped longhouse was home to a married couple and their dependents: men performed outdoor work while women worked indoors. Such houses offered little privacy, though the owner and his wife might have a closet bed. Many dwellings had only one room; the prosperous might have more than one. Sometimes, a separate building was used for the preparation of food, but cooking was often carried out on a separate fire in the main building.

Domestic life was the province of women in the Viking Age. Women looked after the food supply. They were responsible for all aspects of dairying, including the making of butter, cheese, curds, and whey. Men might fish and slaughter cattle, but women prepared the smoked fish and meat for the long winter. Women also took care of meal preparation and the household laundry. Even the wives of important farmers worked at such tasks. For example, in *The Saga of the People of Laxardale*, Gudrun Osvifrsdaughter is occupying herself with the laundry as her husband is murdered. Wool was a vital part of the Icelandic economy and was the basis of its most important domestic industry, the weaving of homespun cloth (*vaðmál*). Homespun cloth was important as an article of inland and overseas trade. Indeed, the value of other items were often expressed in terms of homespun cloth. This industry rested largely on the work of women. Men tended the sheep, but women did the spinning, weaving, and the making of clothes. Manuscript illustrations of Icelandic women show them with spindles and whorls.

CHILDREN

In the Viking Age, boys could inherit at the age of 16, and girls could marry at the age of 12. However, Icelandic law forbade the marriage of those who could not afford to support offspring and specified in detail how the responsibility for dependents fell to relatives in case of need. Pre-Christian law permitted infanticide; indeed, until the thirteenth century, Norway continued to allow the practice in the case of certain extreme disabilities, though baptism was required. The law reflected a society in which survival was a pressing economic problem. The most urgent concern was that everyone should have an adequate means of support. As a guarantee that the indigent should not procreate, Icelandic law permitted the involuntary castration of beggars; the death of the victim as a result of the operation was not regarded as a crime.

The law specified a strict order of inheritance to the advantage of legitimate males. The illegitimate had rights of inheritance but, in Iceland, they came at the end of a long line of legitimate heirs. Given that concubinage was commonplace, even after the coming of Christianity, the pagan custom of infanticide and its survival into Christian times may have a partial explanation in the difficulty of supporting numerous illegitimate children. Norwegian law was less strict; it gave legal standing to the offspring of concubinage if the relationship had been open and stable.

The Lay of Rig depicts childhood as an apprenticeship for adulthood. Only Jarl and his children appear to follow intellectual pursuits of any sort (learning runes, for example). The education of children in the pagan, pre-manuscript period was a function of the family in its communication of custom and tradition. Children learned by doing and imitating. In an age of oral poetry, listening must also have been a way of learning. The survival of some poetry by women skalds suggests that girls were permitted (or possibly encouraged) to participate in oral instruction in the art of poetry.

Literacy is associated with the coming of Christianity, and formal education took place in cathedral and monastic schools, with an emphasis on the preparation of priests. Wealthy Icelandic laymen, such as the Oddverjar and Haukadælir families, ran schools where the children of the gentry could receive an education. Little is known about what was taught, but historical works such as Ari Thorgilsson's *Íslendingabók* may have been used. Olaf Thordarson Hvitaskald (the White Skald; ca 1210–59) was a nephew of Snorri Sturluson (1179–1241) and brother of Sturla Thordarson (1214–84), the historian. Olaf wrote a rhetorical and grammatical handbook, the *Third Grammatical Treatise*, which has all the appearance of an instructional text and is based on the Latin writers Priscian and Donatus. Interestingly, Olaf uses Icelandic texts to illustrate the linguistic and rhetorical features discussed. Given that Latin was the usual language of learning at this time, Olaf's use of Icelandic as the medium of instruction reveals the unusual power of the vernacular tradition in Iceland.

LAW

Early Scandinavian law originated from the practices of local assemblies (things), which met to arrange for defense and the observance of religious rites. Regulation of social practices followed. Eventually, larger regional assemblies emerged such as those regularized by Hakon the Good (r. 935–961) in Norway (Gula-thing, Frostathing). Norwegian regional assemblies were representative, except for the Eyrathing at Trondheim, which required the attendance of every local freeman. The things all had both a legislative and a judicial function; their major weakness was that they lacked any executive to put their decisions into effect.

Justice as handed down by the things was a complex matter. Legal penalties were usually fines based not simply on the nature of the crime committed but also on the *réttr* or worth of the victim. The notion that each individual had a *réttr* (loosely translated as rights or worth) was fundamental to Germanic law. However, these rights were not equal. There was a sliding scale of worth according to an individual's social status. A good illustration of this scale can be found in the introduction to Larson's *The Earliest Norwegian Laws*:

> The scale of "right" in its simplest form is stated in the Gulathing law. In the Gula province a baron [*lendr maðr*, landed man] enjoyed a right of six marks. That of a *hǫldr* was three marks. A common freeman could claim one and one-half marks. A freedman who had given his freedom ale had a right of six oras, or half as much as a freeman. His son, who was further along the road to freedom, was rated at one mark (eight oras). But if the freedman had not given his ale, his right was only four oras. (Larson 1935, 13)

What was the significance of an individual having a *réttr* or price? In the event of a crime, such as wounding or killing, this price would be paid by the offender to the victim (if still alive) or to his family. In Anglo-Saxon England, this concept was termed *wergild* or man-payment. In Scandinavian law, it was referred to as *bauggildi* (ring or money payment) or *nefgildi* (kinsman payment).

Gulathing law also indicates how the rank of the accused was sometimes taken into consideration when determining the severity of the fine:

> 185. Concerning the valuation of wounds: if a freedman wounds a man, he shall pay one *baug* [twelve gold coins]; his son [shall pay] two *baugs*; a freeman, three *baugs*; a man born to odal right, six *baugs*; a baron [*lendr maðr* = landed man] or a staller [*stallari* = royal official, marshal], twelve *baugs*; a jarl, twenty-four *baugs*; and the king, forty-eight *baugs*. (Larson 1935, 139)

It was not only individuals who were ranked by *réttr*. Different parts of the body were also valued according to their perceived worth. In the following instance, the Gulathing law assigns appropriate fines for lost or maimed digits:

> 180. Now a thumb is as dear as all the other [fingers]: a thumb shall be paid for with three marks; the next finger with one mark and the long finger at the same [rate]; the one that is next to it with six oras and the little finger with two oras. (Larson 1935, 138)

Fines and compensation of this sort were the norm. In the sagas, the exact sum and nature of compensation were often matters for complex negotiation. In *Njal's Saga*, negotiations break down at a crucial point; the death of Njal and his sons is a direct consequence of that failure. Capital punishment was carried out by hanging and was a frequent punishment for theft, perhaps on the assumption that a thief would lack the wherewithal to pay a fine.

For offenses involving assault or homicide, the penalty might be outlawry. This punishment was severe, involving exile and loss of property. Lesser outlawry (*fjörbaugsgarðr*) brought exile for three years, together with loss of property, but it guaranteed the exile safe passage from the country. A confiscation court was responsible for overseeing the outlaw's banishment and the disposal of his property. Full outlawry (*skógangr*) denied the outlaw all legal rights and forbade the harboring or assisting of the outlaw in any way, though a special dispensation sometimes allowed the full outlaw safe passage from the land. With a price on his head, the full outlaw might be killed anywhere without penalty, but the lesser outlaw had the usual protection of the law while out of the country. These penalties were harsh but comprehensible in a society without the state mechanisms of prisons and police. They were an effective means of ridding society of habitual offenders.

Words could have as serious consequences as deeds. For example, writing poetry to a woman carried the penalty of lesser outlawry. Full outlawry was the penalty for the following offenses:

> If a man composes a love-verse on a woman, then the penalty is full outlawry.... If a man recites poetry in order to mock someone, even though it was composed about somebody else, or twists some line in it to apply to him, then the penalty is full outlawry. (Dennis, Foote, and Perkins 2000, 198–99)

The use of certain words suggesting a man's lack of virility gave the right to kill:

> 423. There are three expressions, if words between men ever get so bad, for all of which the penalty is full outlawry: if a man calls another man womanish or says he has been buggered or fucked...and in retaliation for those three words, a man also has the right to kill...and the man who says these words falls with forfeit immunity at the hands of all who accompany the man of whom they were said to the place of action. (Dennis, Foote, and Perkins 2000, 354)

While these laws show little regard for freedom of speech, they show a healthy respect for the power of the word.

BOX 2.1 *Place-names and* **Things**

PHOTO 2.1   Tingwall in Shetland. Virtually all of the place-names in the
Orkney and Shetland Islands are Scandinavian in origin, as this road sign from
Tingwall in Shetland illustrates. (Photo by R.A. McDonald)

What do Tingwall in Orkney and Shetland, Tiongal in the Isle of Lewis,
Dingwall in northern Scotland, Thingwall in the Wirral, Cheshire,
and Tynwald in the Isle of Man, have in common? These place-names
are derived from Old Norse Thingvellir (*Þingvöllr*), "Assembly-plain,"
and recall a place where a Scandinavian open-air judicial assembly—a
Þing—was once held. The most famous Viking Age assembly site is
Þingvöllr (often referred to in pl. *Þingvellir*) in Iceland, site of the Althing
(*Alþing*), established in 930. It was held for two weeks at midsummer
and was attended by chieftains from all over the island. Norse settlers
who came to the British Isles brought with them their concept of
the *thing*; these were held at locations that had suitable level ground
for the accommodation of people and horses. There are 11 *Þingvellir*
names in the British Isles. These tell a tale of Scandinavian settlement
and of the extent to which Scandinavian customs took root. Some of
the sites (Law Ting Holm, Tingwall, Shetland; Tynwald Hill, Isle of
Man) preserve physical remains associated with the assemblies, and at
several of these places assemblies continued to be held for centuries.
Tynwald in the Isle of Man, with its four-tiered Tynwald Hill and

processional way to Saint John's church, still hosts an annual meeting of the Manx Parliament on 5 July, a testament to the Norse heritage of the Isle of Man.

PHOTO 2.2 Tynwald Hill, Isle of Man. The place-name Tynwald in the Isle of Man recalls a Norse assembly site on the island. The four-tiered Tynwald Hill (foreground) has been ceremonially significant for centuries; the earliest textual references to it occur in the late Norse period. (Photo by R.A. McDonald)

FORMATION OF STATES

Associating the Vikings with state building may seem paradoxical—after all, they are usually linked with the destruction of kingdoms—but one of the most significant developments of the Viking Age was the creation of unified kingdoms in Denmark, Norway, and Sweden as well as in other parts of the Viking world. The process moved faster in some regions than in others, and geography played an important role in dictating the pace of centralization. At the beginning of the Viking Age, Scandinavia was dominated by small kingdoms or chiefdoms, although by the last period of the Scandinavian Iron Age (roughly 600–800), fairly powerful regional kingdoms had started to emerge around Lake Mälaren in Sweden, in Jutland in Denmark, and in Vestfold in Norway. As the Viking Age progressed, these kingdoms were forged into the medieval states of Denmark, Norway, and Sweden.

We know most about state building in Denmark, where by about 800 the Danes had already created a kingdom that embraced most of modern Denmark, parts of southern Sweden, and the Vestfold region of Norway. The early ninth century was characterized by murderous strife among the members of the Danish royal house, and not until the mid-tenth century did a new and powerful dynasty emerge at Jelling in Jutland to re-establish a unified kingdom of Denmark. Credit for the unification of Denmark is taken by Harald Bluetooth Gormsson, a ruler in Jutland in the middle of the tenth century.

BOX 2.2   *The Royal Monuments at Jelling, Denmark*

Some of the most impressive monuments of the Viking Age in Scandinavia are found at Jelling, on the Jutland Peninsula of Denmark. Two great flat-topped mounds, a church, two runestones, and a stone enclosure date from the second half of the tenth century and are associated with Gorm the Old and his son Harald Bluetooth (see chapter 3), whose achievements they commemorate.

The oldest monuments are King Gorm's stone for his queen, a large stone enclosure that may have represented the outline of a ship, and the North Mound. The stone (140 cm tall) has a runic inscription that reads, "King Gorm made this memorial to his wife Thyrve [or Thyra], glory of Denmark." Its original location is uncertain. The North Mound, 65 m in diameter and 8.5 m in height, is the largest burial mound in Denmark. When excavated in the nineteenth century it was found to contain a timber burial chamber that contained no human remains; only a few objects were recovered, one of them a splendid silver cup. Dendrochronology reveals that the mound was constructed in 958/59, and because this is likely the end of King Gorm's reign, it is believed that he was buried there.

Gorm's son Harald Bluetooth subsequently expanded the monuments. The larger, three-sided runestone, known as King Harald's stone (243 cm tall), has a runic inscription as well as remarkable carvings of a beast and snake on one side and of Christ on another. The inscription reads: "King Harald ordered this monument to be carved in memory of Gorm, his father, and Thyrve [or Thyra] his mother. [This was] the Harald who conquered Denmark and all Norway and made the Danes Christian." The stone sits in its original location halfway between the two mounds. The South Mound, 77 m in diameter and 11 m high, did not contain a burial. It was constructed following the conversion and has been interpreted as a memorial for King Harald, who was buried at Roskilde. Massive stones forming a V-shaped setting were found beneath it, although what they represent remains uncertain: they may have formed part of a ship-outline built in association with the North Mound, but have also been interpreted as part of a sanctuary.

PHOTO 2.3   **Jelling Runestones. (a) The larger of the two runestones at Jelling was raised by King Harald Gormsson Bluetooth in memory of Gorm and Thyrvé (Thyra), his parents, ca 965. (b) The smaller and older runestone at Jelling was erected by King Gorm the Old in memory of his wife Thyrvé (Thyra). (Photo by M. Stephenson)**

Between the mounds stands a Romanesque stone church dating from ca 1100. It was built over three earlier wooden churches, the oldest of which dates from the time of Harald Bluetooth's conversion in the 960s and was larger than the present church. In the 1970s, excavations of this earliest church revealed a grave beneath it. This contained the skeletal remains of a strongly built, middle-aged male who had originally been buried somewhere else and subsequently moved here. Gold threads and two silver gilt strap-ends found in the grave revealed the location from which the bones had been moved: they were closely related to some of the finds from the burial chamber in the North Mound. The bones are therefore thought to be those of Gorm, probably moved from his original pagan burial place in the North Mound and given a retroactive Christian burial by his son Harald sometime after Harald's conversion in the 960s. The whereabouts of Thyra's remains are not known.

> Jelling was a monument begun under the pagan Gorm and subsequently developed into a Christian site after the conversion of Harald in the 960s. Jelling is now on UNESCO's list of World Heritage Sites. The monuments were regrettably vandalized in 2011.

Early ninth-century Norway was divided into a number of chiefdoms and regions, and parts of southern Norway such as Vestfold were under the control of Danish rulers. The medieval Icelandic saga tradition associates the unification of Norway with the king of Vestfold, Harald *hárfagri* (Finehair), at the end of the ninth and beginning of the tenth century, but modern scholarship is now skeptical of these claims. Snorri Sturluson (in his *Heimskringla*; see below) describes Harald's campaigns against a variety of other Norwegian rulers, culminating in his great victory at Hafrsfjorðr (Havsfjord). The dates of his reign are uncertain. His accession is estimated at ca 860–880, his victory at Havsfjord at ca 885–890, and his death at 930–940. Harald's contribution to Norwegian state building is now viewed as much less significant than the Icelandic saga tradition suggests. His hold over the northern and eastern parts of his kingdom was limited at best, and whatever he had accomplished during his lifetime did not survive his death, when his numerous sons (perhaps as many as 20) fell to feuding over their father's revenues and title to the kingship. The saga tradition sees Harald's victory at Havsfjord as a cause of the exodus of chieftains from Norway and the settlement of Iceland. But Ari Thorgilsson the Wise (1067–1148), the author of *The Book of the Icelanders* (*Íslendingabók*), gives no support to this view of Icelandic colonization. Morevoer, the Icelandic land taking began in the mid-870s, a date that is now regarded as far too early for Havsfjord.

In this period, much less is known about Sweden, which was inhabited by two peoples, the Svear and the Götar. The Svear kingdom (from which Sweden takes its name) expanded in the ninth century, and by the end of the tenth and start of the eleventh century one king, Olof Skötkonung (ca 995–1020), ruled both peoples.

Elsewhere in the Scandinavian world, other centralized states emerged, though they were not destined to last much beyond the end of the Viking Age. In Orkney the powerful earls were technically subject to Norway but were formidable rulers in their own right, particularly through the eleventh century. In the Hebrides and in the Isle of Man, dynasties of sea-kings of Norse origin arose during the eleventh and twelfth centuries. At the same time, loose "Viking empires" emerged briefly in the North Sea and Irish Sea: the eleventh-century earls of Orkney are said to have controlled Orkney, parts of Scotland, the Hebrides, and perhaps the Isle of Man; King Cnut the Great (d. 1035), a grandson of Harald Bluetooth, ruled England, Denmark, Norway, and, perhaps, part of Sweden.

State building, particularly in Denmark, Norway, and Sweden, is inseparable from the conversion to Christianity. For the most part, the kings who unified their kingdoms were also Christian and were responsible for converting their respective peoples, as King Harald Bluetooth of Denmark, for instance, boasted on his runestone at Jelling. In Norway, Christianization had little place, so far as we can tell, in Harald Finehair's agenda, but Harald's role in state building there is downplayed by modern scholars who point instead to Olaf Tryggvason and Olaf Haraldsson (Saint Olaf) as being responsible for creating a strong unitary kingship. The fact that these so-called Vikings for Christ were also state builders is not a coincidence, since they, like Harald Bluetooth and others, recognized the potential of Christianity, both in terms of doctrine and church organization, as a means to strengthen kingship and promote unity.

THE SPECIAL CASE OF ICELAND

Icelandic political and legal practices owed much to Norway and the institution of the assembly or *Thing*. When Norwegians first colonized Iceland, they brought the *Thing* with them, but not monarchy. Though Norwegian kings had a proprietorial attitude toward Iceland, the country remained independent until 1262; it is customary to refer to Icelandic society from 930 until absorption by Norway as the Icelandic Commonwealth (or Free State). The early settlers of Iceland were a relatively homogenous group: none were exceptionally rich, and none exceptionally poor. While inequalities doubtless existed, there was a fairly uniform landed interest. The settlers who arrived early established large land takes, which they divided among their followers and late-comers.

The most prominent among the early settlers established themselves as local chieftains (*goði*, pl. *goðar*). The office of the *goði* was known as a *goðorð*. Originally, the *goðar* numbered 36, though that number increased later. The early history of assemblies is not clear, but the first stage was likely the establishment of regional assemblies, each presided over by as many as three local *goðar*. With the establishment of a national assembly, the Althing (*alþing*), in 930, an Icelandic constitution took shape. Local assemblies were to meet in the spring for the discussion of local business and the trial of lawsuits. Business that affected the whole country and lawsuits not settled by the spring assemblies were dealt with at the Althing in June. Decisions of the Althing were announced at regional assemblies in the autumn.

The Althing was attended by all the *goðar*, accompanied by their followers, known as thingmen (*þingmen*), all of them free farmers. Iceland's only state

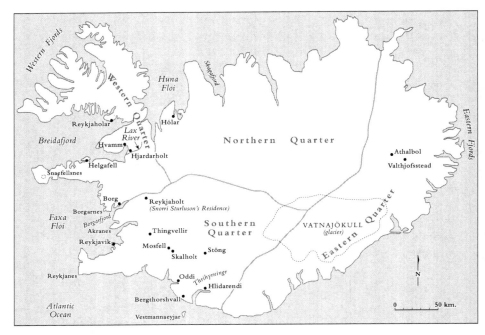

MAP 2.1 **Viking Age Iceland**

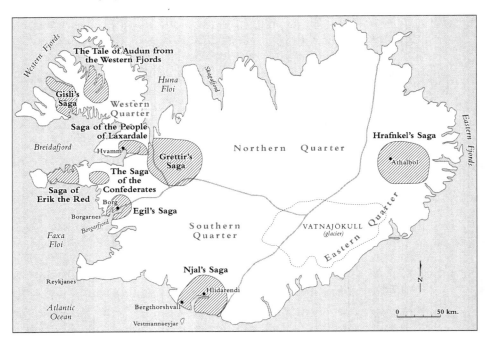

MAP 2.2 **Iceland of the Sagas**

appointee was the Lawspeaker (*lögsögumaðr*), who was elected for a three-year term. Among his duties, he was required to recite a third of the laws at the Althing in each year of his term. He was also expected to answer questions about the law. The legislative and judicial heart of the Althing was the *lögrétta* (legislature) over which the Lawspeaker presided. Only *goðar* were permitted to vote at the *lögrétta*, at which they were accompanied by two advisers from the ranks of their thingmen.

During the 960s, the system was reformed. Often local assemblies proved unable to settle lawsuits, especially when plaintiff and defendant belonged to different regions. In such cases, impartiality could not be guaranteed. In fact, when one notoriously divisive case was referred to the Althing, serious fighting broke out. The solution was to divide the country into quarters, each, except the Northern Quarter, having nine *goðar* and three local assemblies. The Northern Quarter was more populous and larger than the other quarters, so three extra *goðar* were appointed to preside over an additional local assembly. A Quarter Court for each quarter was established at the Althing, and these courts dealt with unresolved lawsuits from each quarter. The Quarter Court soon became the preferred setting for most important local suits. Nine additional *goðar* with limited authority were appointed to preserve the regional balance at the Althing, disturbed by the appointment of additional *goðar* in the Northern Quarter. Final additions to the ranks of the *goðar* were the bishops of Skalholt and Hólar.

The Quarter Courts proved unable to settle everything. In consequence, a Fifth Court was established early in the eleventh century to hear cases not resolved by the Quarter Courts. Effectively, the Fifth Court was a court of appeal.

The Althing met for two weeks in June at Thingvellir (Thing-plain), near Reykjavík in southwest Iceland. Apart from a farm and, later, two churches, there were no permanent buildings on Thingvellir. The chieftains maintained semi-permanent residences (*búð*, pl. *búðir*), consisting of turf walls that were roofed with homespun cloth for every June meeting.

All meetings of the *lögrétta* were held in the open air, as were sessions of the various courts. Legislation and justice were governed by established procedures, transparent, and entirely open to public view. Though only *goðar* might vote, considerable numbers of freemen attended as thingmen of the chieftains. The result was a large body of publicly (though not democratically) approved legislation. The sagas of Icelanders often use meetings of the Althing as a dramatic setting. *Njal's Saga* is particularly focused on the procedural complexities of the Althing. *The Saga of the Confederates* (*Bandamanna saga*) cynically narrates the ease with which the institution could be corrupted.

Iceland had a legislature and judiciary, but no executive branch. Effectively, this privatized justice; after judgment was passed, enforcement was left in the

PHOTO 2.4 Thingvellir, the site of the Icelandic Althing (National Assembly), established in 930. (Photo by R.A. McDonald)

hands of the plaintiff. A major function of the *goðar* was, in fact, to make sure that judgments were executed. A *goði* who proved inadequate to the task would find that his thingmen were likely to vote with their feet.

This system of government was unique and worked relatively well until the twelfth and thirteenth centuries, when too much power fell into the hands of a few prominent families. The resulting civil war rendered Iceland ungovernable; the consequent collapse of civil society made the submission of Iceland to Hakon IV of Norway unavoidable. *The Saga of the Sturlungs* (*Sturlunga saga*) is a gripping account of the last years of the Icelandic Commonwealth.

EARLY RELIGION AND BELIEF

What is known about Norse religion must be inferred from the surviving mythology, the evidence of the saga-literature, the work of early historians such as Adam of Bremen, and the archaeological record. It is important to remember that mythology is a poor guide to religious practice. Do myths evolve as explanations of ritual, or is ritual inspired by belief as expressed in mythology? Inference is problematic in either direction. So Scandinavian mythology requires a careful and nuanced approach. As for the saga-literature, it cannot be relied upon as an accurate depiction of pre-Christian times, since it received written form long after the disappearance of paganism. The same holds true for Adam of Bremen, who was a Christian with no direct knowledge of pagan practices. Finally, the archaeological record is not clear and unambiguous; it requires careful interpretation.

Our knowledge of Norse mythology depends heavily on the work of the thirteenth-century Icelander Snorri Sturluson, whose *Edda* is an extraordinary compilation of myth and poetry. Without it, what we know about the subject would be seriously diminished. A second source for Norse myth and religion is the late thirteenth-century Icelandic manuscript known as the Codex Regius (King's Book, *Konungsbók*), which anthologizes heroic and mythological Norse poems known collectively as *The Poetic Edda*. Many of the poems are probably considerably older than the manuscript. Without these sources and accounts in various sagas and histories, the world of Norse paganism would be largely lost to us.

Snorri was a Christian who wrote more than two centuries after the conversion of Iceland. While he may have had access to a manuscript anthology very much like the Codex Regius from which to draw the bulk of his mythological material, it is possible that Snorri encountered the poems in oral versions. His collecting of myths was driven by his desire to preserve the knowledge and composition of skaldic poetry, which relied for much of its diction on the Norse mythology ousted by Christianity. The fruits of his research is his *Edda* (sometimes known as *The Younger* or *Prose Edda*). The *Edda* is essentially an account of the art of skaldic poetry in three parts. The first, *The Tricking of Gylfi* (*Gylfaginning*), recasts in prose dialogue a series of myths stretching from creation to Ragnarök—the death of the gods and the end of the world—followed by the emergence of a new world. A poetic version of much of this material appears in the first poem of *The Poetic Edda*, *The Prophecy of the Seeress* (*Völuspá*); *Gylfaginning* is marked by frequent direct quotation from the poem. Such myths are a major source of the complex imagery employed by the skalds.

The second part of *Edda*, *Poetic Diction* (*Skáldskaparmál*), preserves more myths and illustrates their use in poetry by extensive quotation from the works of the skalds. The *List of Meters* (*Háttatal*), the third part, is a discussion of skaldic verse-forms, largely illustrated by a poem composed by Snorri himself. Both of these use dialogue form.

Snorri's "Prologue" to the *Edda* euhemerizes the pagan gods (i.e., treats their legends as accounts of historical persons), representing them as great leaders with magical knowledge who came to be regarded as gods by superstitious Scandinavians. This is a perfectly understandable way for a medieval Christian writer to salvage a mythology that was culturally necessary to him. To his credit, Snorri generally stands clear of his material and appears to allow the stories to speak for themselves. In this, he recalls the *Beowulf*-poet, another

Christian writer (of the Anglo-Saxon period) who can treat the pagan past without intrusive moralizing.

Another source of information is found in sagas of various kinds, which also date from the thirteenth century or later. The sagas of Icelanders offer glimpses of pagan practices, but not in any systematic way. Moreover, the historical reliability of the sagas of Icelanders is debatable; the most that may be said, perhaps, is that these sagas have a certain plausibility, created partly by overlapping among the sagas, and partly by confirmation of some details by reliable historical sources. Several sagas that record the lives of kings include descriptions of pagan religious practices, usually at the moment of their eradication by the king in question. Some of these sagas are found in Snorri's *Heimskringla*, a history of the kings of Norway, while Snorri's sagas of Olaf Tryggvason and Saint Olaf offer dramatic accounts of the nature and destruction of paganism. Snorri used earlier written material, and *Heimskringla* was written long after the events recorded.

Christian historians such as Adam of Bremen (fl. late eleventh century) and Saxo Grammaticus (ca 1150–1220) are yet another source. Not surprisingly, they are unsympathetic in their treatment of Germanic and Norse paganism. For example, Adam gives a grisly account of sacrifices at Uppsala.

Despite the apparent richness of the sources, an understanding of Norse paganism is beset by many uncertainties. For example, are the thirteenth-century sources eclectic in bundling together material from different times and places? Does Snorri give an account of Norse belief as it existed at any single moment or place? The Norse left a vocabulary naming their gods and several of their religious practices and feasts, but they left no name for their religion itself, if they ever used such a name, and their religion was labeled *heathen* or *pagan* by the followers of the new faith. Does this lack of a single name suggest that Snorri's systematic treatment of the mythology gives a false impression of unity, of an organized body of religious myth and practice that simply never existed?

Furthermore, textual sources are not helpful in establishing a chronology of Norse religion. For instance, our thirteenth-century texts describe several ways of disposing of the dead: ship burial, burial in mounds, burial in graves, and cremation. One non-Norse Germanic text, *Beowulf*, includes at least three sets of funerary practices. The texts present us with a common mythological time, rather than a developmental chronology, which might explain the variety of customs. Also, there are hints that Odin was not always the chief god and there are references to a war between the Æsir and another race of gods, the Vanir. Indeed, our sources give only tantalizing hints of a history of Norse religion and myth. The Roman historian Tacitus, for instance, suggests in his

Germania (ca 100 CE) that Germanic worship took place in sacred woods and groves, yet Adam of Bremen describes a splendid temple at Uppsala. When and how did temples develop, if at all? These questions suggest that our textual sources ignore the evolution of Norse mythology and religion.

Tacitus suggests that human sacrifice was a part of Germanic religion, and some sagas do contain references to the practice. In the tenth century, the Arab traveler Ibn Fadlan describes what was probably a Norse ship crema-tion in Russia. His account indicates that the ceremony included the sacrifice of a girl, sent to accompany her lord. The Oseberg ship burial contains two female corpses, but we cannot be absolutely certain that one was sacrificed. The picture stone Stora Hammars I, in Gotland, displays motifs suggestive of the worship of Odin; part of one scene may show a human sacrifice. Although the archaeological record is suggestive, human sacrifice is hard to prove, and the presence of more than one body in a burial is not absolutely conclusive; a husband and wife may have been buried in the same grave at different times. Even signs of violent death are not certain evidence. In some cases, the victim may have been an executed criminal. While the case for human sacrifice is unclear, the case for animal sacrifice is stronger. Both saga evidence and the evidence of ship burials suggest that animal sacrifice was part of Norse pagan culture and that it was carried out by local chieftains to propitiate the gods and invoke their help.

Archaeology shows that cremation was widespread in early Scandinavia, as was burial, and that burial of corpses and ashes often involved the deposit of grave goods with the dead. Grave goods perhaps indicated the status of the dead, or were thought to travel with him or her to a next world; either, or both, may be the case, but archaeology cannot decide the question for us. Cremation declined with the coming of Christianity, as did the burial of grave goods. Archaeology suggests that funerary practices varied both regionally and chronologically before the coming of Christianity.

The evidence of place-names indicates that the cults of various members of the Norse pantheon had a regional distribution. Denmark, for instance, is rich in place-names based on Týr and Odin, both of them war gods. Norway, on the other hand, has more names based on fertility gods such as Thor and Freyr. Sweden cultivated both Odin and Freyr. Recent scholarship suggests that this regional distribution has a chronological dimension, with worship of fertility gods representing the religion of the earliest period of settlement.

All of the evidence (whether mythological, archaeological, or historical) must therefore be treated with caution. Myths are stories about gods, not theology; histories must be read in the context of their own cultures; and the archaeological record requires careful interpretation.

The Principal Gods of Norse Mythology and Their World

Norse mythology presents us with a world of dramatic landscapes, inhabited by gods and giants with very human characteristics and by a variety of fearsome monsters. In the beginning, all that existed was Ginnunga Gap, the Great Void, which was cold in the north and fiery in the south. From the meeting of fire and ice, drops of moisture developed, and this moisture produced life in the form of the giant, Ymir. Eventually, the Norse world was created by the act of Odin and his brothers when they killed Ymir, forming the sky from his skull, the sea from his blood, and the earth from his flesh and bones.

In this world, the gods (*Æsir*) inhabit Asgard (*Ásgarðr*, enclosure, home of the gods), which is linked to Midgard (*Miðgarðr*, middle enclosure, Middle Earth) by Bifröst, the trembling bridge or rainbow. Surrounding Midgard is a sea where the World Serpent (*Miðgarðsormr, Jörmungandr*) dwells, and beyond the sea is Utgard (*Útgarðar*, Outer Lands), the home of the giants. Utgard is also known as Jötunheim (*Jötunheimar*, the Worlds of the Giants). Beneath Midgard is the underworld Niflheim, the Land of Mists, which is the residence of those who die in bed or of sickness. It is ruled over by the goddess Hel, daughter of Loki and the giantess Angrboda. At the center of the universe grows the world-tree, Yggdrasil (Odin's Horse), so called because Odin was hanged there as the price for gaining wisdom. The roots of the tree spread to all the worlds of the universe.

Against this backdrop, gods and giants scheme, fight, form alliances, and shift allegiances as they battle for supremacy. The major protagonists are listed in box 2.3.

BOX 2.3   *Major Gods and Giants of Norse Mythology*

1. Æsir: the main tribe of gods in the Norse pantheon. They inhabit Asgard (Ásgarðr: literally, enclosure of the gods).

   Odin, Óðinn: he is the ruler of Asgard and a major but complex god. On the one hand, he is the god of wisdom, poetry, and war. On the other hand, he is a shape-shifter who dabbles in the magical art (seiðr), an art generally confined to women and thought to emasculate men. Odin is the god of warriors and aristocrats but he is also associated with frenzy and the berserkers' rage. He is well known for his band of warrior maidens, the Valkyries, who convey the heroic dead (einherjar) to Valhalla. His attributes are a magical spear, Gungnir, and an eight-legged

---

horse, Sleipnir. He is one-eyed and is accompanied by two ravens (Hugin, Thought; and Munin, Memory).

Frigg: wife of Odin and mother of Baldur.

Baldur, Baldr: a son of Odin noted for his beauty. His death signals the beginning of the process that ends with Ragnarök, the Doom of the Gods.

Thor, Þórr: another of Odin's sons, he is the mightiest of the gods, the defender of Asgard, the killer of giants and the protector of men. Thor is the god of farmers and sailors. He is associated with thunder, the weather, and fertility. His major attribute is the hammer, Mjölnir.

Loki: the son of a goddess and a giant. With the giantess Angrboða he fathers the goddess Hel, the wolf Fenrir, and the World-Serpent Jörmungandr. In the guise of a mare, he gives birth to Odin's eight-legged horse, Sleipnir. Although Loki is sometimes a helper of the gods, he is also a trouble-maker who is responsible for the death of Odin's son, Baldur.

Týr: a one-handed god associated with battle. He may have been the original ruler of the pantheon.

Heimdallr: he is the watchman of the gods who, in the poem Rígsþula, is said to have created the human social order. His status is ambiguous, however. He may belong to the Vanir.

2. Vanir: a group of gods associated with fertility. The Vanir fought the first ever war with the Æsir. While it is not clear if either side won decisively, the Vanir appear to have been absorbed by the Æsir

Freyja: goddess of love, beauty, fertility and magic. In one source, she welcomes half the heroic dead at her home, Fólkvangr. Her attributes include a chariot drawn by two cats, and the necklace Brísingamen.

Freyr: a fertility god associated with weather and farming. He marries the giantess Gerðr. His attributes are Gullinbursti, a golden boar, and Skiðblaðnir, a ship that can be folded up and carried in a pouch.

Njörðr: a fertility god whose home by the sea signals his association with fishing and seafaring. He has an incestuous relationship with his sister and fathers Freyja and Freyr.

3. Giants: In Norse mythology, the term for giant is Jötunn, Risi, or Þurs: a Mountain-giant is Bergrisi; a Frost-giant is Hrímþurs.

> Ymir: the first living being, ancestor of the Frost-giants. From his body, Odin and his sons created the world.
>
> Hymir: a giant who fished with Thor for the World-Serpent. Hymir was overcome by terror at the sight of the serpent and cut Thor's fishing line.
>
> Surtr: the leader of the Fire-giants who destroys the world at Ragnarök.
>
> Suttungr: the giant from whom Odin steals the mead of poetry.
>
> Angrboða: the giantess by whom Loki produces his monstrous family.

In Norse mythology, Odin creates an orderly world, while Loki's creations are monstrous and destructive. Loki, who is the son of a goddess and a giant, personifies a fundamental instability of the Norse universe. While gods may marry down (Odin had a giantess for a mother), giants are not expected to marry up. Thus Loki is not strictly one of the Æsir, though he lives with and often cooperates with them. At other times, he acts with malice, as when he arranges the murder of Odin's son, Baldur. Loki has the giants' elemental destructiveness, as do his monstrous offspring. The conflict between Odin's rational creativity and the monstrosity of the giants comes to an end in the last battle when Loki and Hel lead the giants against the gods. In the course of this battle, Odin is swallowed by the wolf Fenrir, and Thor is killed by the World-Serpent.

It is important to remember that what we know of Norse mythology and religion was largely preserved long after Christian influence had begun to make itself felt in Scandinavia. Even a text as heavily pagan as *The Prophecy of the Seeress* shows clear signs of Christian influence. The account of Ragnarök, for example, has strong echoes of the Christian book of Revelation.

CONVERSION

In the popular imagination, Vikings are militant pagans, hostile to Christianity. This view is understandable enough, given their apparent predilection for sacking churches and monasteries. In fact, the Vikings were by no means anti-Christian; rather, they were drawn to churches and monasteries because these places were repositories of portable wealth and easy sources of captives and slaves. Viking religion was not intolerant or aggressive, and it was entirely possible to make room for Christ alongside traditional deities such as Odin and Thor: we are told, for example, in *Egil's Saga* that Helgi the Lean, an early settler of Iceland, had been baptized as a Christian but "vowed to Thor for sea journeys and difficult undertakings." Then, too, there is the incorrigible pagan Egil Skallagrimsson, a devotee of Odin who, before signing on as a mercenary with King Athelstan of England, accepted the sign of the cross, "as was the general custom then for merchants and mercenaries who associated with Christians, because men who had received the sign of the cross could mix freely with Christians and heathens alike, but could retain whatever faith they pleased." (Egil's Saga, ch. 50. Tr. Scudder in Hreinsson, v. 1)

Before the start of the Viking Age, Scandinavians would have encountered Christianity through avenues such as commerce and diplomacy. Diplomatic contact is hinted at in Rimbert's *Life of Anskar*, where we learn that the Danish king Harald Klak accepted baptism in 826 as part of his political relationship with the Carolingian ruler Louis the Pious. Contact with Christianity intensified during the Viking Age as Scandinavians raided and settled in Christian Europe. Diplomatic agreements, mercenary activities, commercial transactions, land settlement and marriages, the ransoming of people and precious goods—all these required communication and interaction. It should not come as a surprise that conversion to Christianity forms a major theme of the Viking Age, one that cuts across what we have described as the "first" and "second" Viking Ages and represents continuity across some four centuries of Northern history.

The conversion of the Scandinavians was a lengthy and complicated process that spanned several centuries. It occurred earlier in some regions than others, and moved at different paces in different parts of the Viking world. Richard Fletcher (1998, 416) has described the whole process as "gradual, piecemeal, muddled and undisciplined." As an example, the pagan cult at Uppsala in Sweden flourished until the second half of the eleventh century. It lasted for more than a century after King Harald Bluetooth of Denmark proclaimed in the 960s that he had "made the Danes Christian"—and that statement itself was made more than a century after some of Harald's predecessors had accepted Christianity in the course of their dealings with the Carolingian rulers. By the twelfth century, the process of conversion had run its course in most parts of the Scandinavian world, and the Vikings had joined the club of Christian European peoples. An early twelfth-century Norwegian king, Sigurd Magnusson, was known as *Jorsalfari*, or Jerusalem-farer, after his pilgrimage to the Holy Land (1108–10), in the course of which he participated in the capture of Sidon by Crusaders. The circle had closed: Vikings had become Crusaders, and those who had once attacked churches and monasteries had become soldiers of Christ.

PHOTOS 2.5 A AND B Thorwald's Cross, Isle of Man. Tenth-century carved memorial stone from Kirk Andreas in the Isle of Man. On one face (a), a scene from Norse mythology depicts Odin (with raven and spear) being devoured by the wolf Fenrir, part of Ragnarök, the Norse end of the world. The opposite face (b) displays an image that might represent the triumph of Christianity. The Isle of Man is home to a large corpus of unique carved stones. (Photos by R.A. McDonald)

The gradual nature of the conversion presents problems for those attempting to understand it. One difficulty is the nature of the sources. There is no coherent contemporary narrative of the conversion of the Northern peoples, no Scandinavian equivalent of Bede's *Ecclesiastical History of the English People*. In fact, there are few contemporary Scandinavian sources, and those that do exist come from Christian writers such as Rimbert or Adam of Bremen, outsiders looking in, and therefore hardly unbiased observers. Adam of Bremen, for example, wrote as much to extol the claims of the archbishops of Hamburg-Bremen as to provide a narrative account of events. What Scandinavian sources there are were largely composed long after conversion, though this does not automatically make them untrustworthy: Ari Thorgilsson, who wrote *The Book of Icelanders* (*Íslendingabók*) in the early twelfth century, over a century after the conversion of the Icelanders, had as informants native Icelanders whose memories spanned most of the eleventh century. And what are we to make of the sagas of Olaf Tryggvason and Olaf Haraldsson (Saint Olaf) composed by Snorri Sturluson in the middle of the thirteenth century?

A related problem is that texts are unevenly distributed across the Viking world. Sources for the conversion are sparse in places such as Ireland, Scotland, Normandy, Russia, and Greenland, while in Scandinavia itself, Denmark and Norway are better documented than Sweden. Another problem is the nature of conversion as a whole: how far was conversion a conversion of conscience? Conversion and Christianization could be two different things, and the motives of rulers such as Harald Bluetooth of Denmark and Olaf Tryggvason and Olaf Haraldsson of Norway in promoting Christianity in their realms remain open to discussion. The coercive and violent methods used by these rulers have attracted the attention of scholars, one of whom has memorably described Olaf Haraldsson (Saint Olaf) as a "Viking for Christ" in reference to his brutal methods of dealing with religious/political opponents (Cusack 1998).

Conversion and state building were closely connected during the Viking Age and have been used, individually and together, as convenient markers of the end of the Viking Age. While conversion to Christianity in particular led to the assimilation of the Scandinavians into the mainstream of European Christian culture, the examples of Olaf Tryggvason and Olaf Haraldsson caution against the conclusion that conversion to Christianity altered Viking behavior profoundly.

CHAPTER THREE

VIKING BIOGRAPHIES

There is precious little evidence on which to base biographies of Viking Age personalities. Even for members of the elite, basic details such as precise dates of birth and death often elude us—witness the frequent use of ca (circa = about), even for the reigns of kings. The very existence of some individuals whose lives are recorded only in saga narratives may be doubted. For example, Freydis Eiriksdaughter is regarded by some as a literary invention, the antithesis of the virtuous Gudrid Thorbjarnardaughter.

Nevertheless, the Viking Age is full of memorable and sometimes outrageous personalities, some of whom, such as Egil Skallagrimsson, represent the diversity of the age. Egil begins the Viking biographies for this reason, and because the saga bearing his name is generally regarded as one of the finest of the sagas of Icelanders.

Here we present eight brief pen-portraits of individuals from the Viking Age in order to give a sense of the richness and diversity of the period. Many individuals could have been chosen as subjects; our selection strives to achieve chronological, geographical, and social breadth. Our subjects span the Viking world from North America to the eastern Mediterranean, and include kings, outlaws, explorers, settlers, and poets, both male and female. In addition to the figures profiled here, see also the discussions of the Norwegian chieftain Ohthere (chapter 4) and the Viking warlord Weland (box 1.3).

EGIL SKALLAGRIMSSON (CA 910–990): WARRIOR, MERCENARY, POET

Egil Skallagrimsson appears in several Icelandic texts, but he is best known as the eponymous hero of *Egil's Saga*. An examination of the structure of his saga will enrich our understanding of what Egil means in his context and provide an insight into the historicity (or lack of it) of his career. Though the saga is often described as a "poet's saga," it does not follow the others in their emphasis on unfulfilled, romantic love. Egil marries out of love and duty to his dead brother, rather than attachment to his future wife, his brother's widow.

Egil's Saga differs from most of the sagas of Icelanders (see chapter 4) in that the first 27 chapters take place in Norway, long before Egil's birth in Iceland. Harald Finehair's wars in Norway and his final victory at Havsfjord are narrated in detail, in the manner of a king's saga (see chapter 4). Egil's grandfather, Kveldulf, loses his favorite son, Thorolf, to Harald's ambition and jealousy. Thorolf's death introduces the long-lasting enmity between the families of Harald and Kveldulf, an enmity that unfolds in a series of vengeful murders. For instance, Egil murders a grandson of Harald Finehair later in the saga. No historical sources acknowledge anything at all about the involvement of Egil's family in Norwegian politics.

A similar pattern occurs in the next generation, when another Thorolf (favorite son of Skallagrim Kveldulfsson and brother of Egil) is killed at the battle of Brunanburh in England in 937. Later, Egil loses his own favorite son to death by drowning. This generational emphasis on the loss of beloved sons draws attention to the pattern of events, and away from the figure of the hero.

The middle of the saga again differs from most sagas of Icelanders by being located outside Iceland. Egil undertakes raids in the Baltic and leads part of the Anglo-Saxon army at the Battle of Brunanburh in England. Again, there is no historical record of the participation of Egil and his brother, Thorolf, in this battle, which is mentioned in the *Anglo-Saxon Chronicle*.

The construction of Egil's character forms part of an evolving pattern in the saga. His grandfather, Kveldulf, has uncanny qualities; his birth name, Ulf, was modified by the addition of *Kveld* (evening) because those around him believed that he was a shape-shifter who became a wolf by night. Skallagrim, Egil's father, bald, surly, and troll-like, is given to rages of berserk intensity, in one of which he comes close to killing Egil. Skallagrim's strength waxes and wanes with the time of day. Egil inherits his father's appearance and propensity to violence; he commits his first murder at eight years of age and celebrates the event with a poem. He is uncannily adept in the runic arts, and his curses drive Eirik Bloodax from the Norwegian throne. In each of the two generations after Kveldulf, an ugly, dark son contrasts with a blond, distinguished elder brother called Thorolf. Both Thorolfs die a glorious youthful death in battle. In contrast, Skallagrim and Egil live on into a sad and bitter old age.

Indeed, Egil is a grotesquely violent contrast to his uncle and brother. Duels and fights with berserks are standard fare for Norse warriors in the sagas, and Egil has his share. The details of Egil's violence are often nauseating. Biting out the throat of an opponent, the gouging out of eyes, and the tearing out of beards are a few of Egil's violent exploits. The use of projectile vomiting in a fight seems unique to him. The violence of this saga has less in common with other sagas of Icelanders than with the so-called contemporary sagas of the Icelandic civil wars (see chapter 4).

Egil's crude violence is often regarded as an astonishing contrast with the poet who produced the elegy *Sonatorrek* (*The Terrible Loss of Sons*; see below). However, it is important to remember that Odin was a god of war and poetry, and that Egil had always been his follower. Odin was also the master of the runes, a shape-shifter, and a magician. The berserk rage was cultivated by his warriors. From this point of view, neither the variety of Egil's behavior nor the intensity of his violence is surprising.

Egil's Saga contains the work of the finest of skaldic poets. Many scholars attribute these poems to Egil and regard them as the orally transmitted framework of his saga. Others regard the poems as being unusually closely tied to the narrative and composed as part of the saga in the thirteenth century. *Sonatorrek*, in particular, embodies a breath-taking versatility. Is *Sonatorrek* an autobiographical elegy, or an elegy that the author thought appropriate to his construction of Egil? The saga contains three long poems, of which *Sonatorrek* is one, and many short poems. The other two long poems in the saga are *Arinbjarnarkviða* (*Poem for Arinbjorn*), dedicated to his friend Arinbjorn, which is incomplete, and *Höfuðlausn* (*Head-Ransom*), an unusual rhyming poem in praise of Eirik Bloodax. The title of *Höfuðlausn* refers to the origin of the poem: Egil had fallen into the hands of his mortal enemy, Eirik, and composed this poem overnight to save himself from execution. Many of the poems, especially *Sonatorrek*, are works of rhetorical genius.

Bjarni Einarsson (2003) ascribes authorship of the saga *and* of the poems to Snorri Sturluson, the thirteenth-century historian and poet. Snorri's best-known poem is *Háttatal*, a clavis metrica (list of meters) in the form of a praise poem dedicated to Hakon Hakonarson, king of Norway, and Earl Skúli, his co-regent. *Háttatal* is never less than competent, but it fails to match the excellence of the poetry in *Egil's Saga*. The last few poems in the saga are sad reflections on the fate of a blind, deaf, old man.

The historical Egil was born at Borg, in Iceland, at the end of the first decade of the tenth century and died in Iceland ca 990. The structure of his saga suggests the novel rather than the biography form and highlights the problems of historicity raised by many of the sagas of Icelanders.

HARALD BLUETOOTH, KING OF DENMARK (R. CA 958–987)

Harald Gormsson "Bluetooth" was the son of Gorm "the Old" and Thyrve (or Thyra), "the pride of Denmark." He was the father of Svein Forkbeard and the grandfather of Cnut; Svein (d. 1014) and Cnut (d. 1035) conquered England in the early eleventh century. On the large runestone at Jelling, a royal site in Jutland associated with Gorm and Harald (see box 2.2 and photo 2.3), Harald boasted that he won for himself all Denmark and Norway and made the Danes Christian. The precise meaning of this is far from clear, but it stands nevertheless as a statement of how Harald viewed his achievements. There is evidence that a single kingdom of Denmark existed in the eighth century, but this waned and collapsed by the end of the century. Gorm and Harald restored royal authority in Denmark and consolidated power in the hands of a mighty dynasty. Harald's kingdom probably embraced Jutland, Fyn, and Sjaelland in modern Denmark, the southernmost part of modern Sweden (Skåne and Halland), and the area around the Oslofjord in Norway.

Harald was an aggressive warrior king. He intervened in Norwegian affairs, probably ruled the Viken area of Norway, and may have held overlordship of much of the rest of the country. His reign was also characterized by struggles with the German empire to the south, and he was active against the Wends along the south Baltic coast. His wife was a Wendish princess.

Harald's father, Gorm, is depicted in some hostile sources as an incorrigible pagan and persecutor of Christians. The German chronicler Widukind preserves the story of Harald's conversion to Christianity and his baptism at the hands of the missionary Poppo, who allegedly underwent trial by fire to prove the might of the Christian God (ca 965). But Denmark's close contacts with the rest of Europe mean that Christianity can hardly have been unknown there. Missionaries had been active in Denmark for some 200 years by the mid-tenth century, and Christianity was also transmitted through commercial and diplomatic contacts with Carolingian Europe and through connections with the Danish settlements in England. Several Danish bishops are recorded in the 940s, although it is doubtful that they established sees or visited Denmark. Adam of Bremen relates that Christianity was imposed on Harald and the Danes after their defeat by the German emperor, and many modern scholars argue that the Christianization of Denmark was the result of German dominance in the mid-tenth century. Whatever the case, Harald was the first

Scandinavian ruler actively to promote Christianity, and Adam of Bremen depicts him as a model Christian king.

Harald is renowned for the construction of the monumental public works that symbolize his power. Apart from the royal site at Jelling, many fortifications were constructed, including extensions and upgrades to the Danevirke at the base of the Jutland peninsula in the 950s and 960s. Harald also had a series of circular fortresses built in the 980s at Trelleborg in Sjaelland, Fyrkat in east Jutland, Aggersborg in north Jutland, Nonnebakken on Fyn, and possibly Trelleborg in Skåne (modern Sweden). Their scale reveals the considerable resources at Harald's disposal; the largest, Aggersborg in Jutland, is 240 m in diameter, while Trelleborg is 134 m in diameter. The purpose of these fortresses is uncertain, and they were in use for only a short time. Harald's reign also saw the construction of roads and bridges, including a 700-m-long and 6-m-wide timber bridge at Ravning Enge near Jelling in ca 980. The monumental, prestige architecture of the reign distinguishes Harald as a new type of ruler in Denmark.

The end of Harald's reign was characterized by conflict with his son Svein. Sources disagree on the nature of Harald's death, but he probably died of wounds received in a battle with Svein. He was buried at Roskilde rather than at Jelling, where it is thought that the south mound may be a cenotaph for this remarkable king of Denmark.

The origin of Harald's epithet, Bluetooth, is not contemporary and its meaning is uncertain; it may refer to dental problems, to his complexion, or perhaps to the practice revealed by recent discoveries of Scandinavian skulls with grooves filed into the front teeth, which may have been colored.

OLAF TRYGGVASON, KING OF NORWAY (R. 995–1000)

Succession to the Norwegian throne was an uncertain and risky business until the time of Hakon Hakonarson (d. 1263), whose son Magnus inherited without contest, testimony to Hakon's great success in forging a stable state in Norway. Before Hakon, the laws of succession were unclear and, such as they were, seldom observed.

In the tenth and early eleventh centuries, proof of descent from Harald Finehair was the prime qualification for would-be kings of Norway. When Olaf Tryggvason was born, the throne was in the hands of the sons of Eirik Bloodax and his wife, Gunnhild. Harald Greycloak Eiriksson (d. 970) had won the title of king and, in 961, was recognized by Harald Bluetooth, king of Denmark. Harald Greycloak's rule did not extend much beyond western Norway. He attempted to improve his position by murdering petty kings and chieftains who might oppose him. Among his victims was Tryggvi Olafsson, king of Viken in Norway (d. 963). Tryggvi was also a grandson of Harald Finehair and might make claims of his own. Olaf Tryggvason was reputedly the posthumous son of Tryggvi by his wife, Astrid. Since Olaf could claim descent from Harald Finehair, he too was seen as a potential threat by Harald Greycloak, whose failed attempts to kill the infant drove Astrid into exile and began the tumultuous adventures that were the life of Olaf Tryggvason.

Astrid's brother, Sigurd, was in the service of Valdemar, king of Gardariki (Russia). In an attempt to join him, she and her infant son were captured by pirates in the Baltic and sold into slavery. Olaf never forgot the pirate who killed his foster-father as being too old for a slave; long afterwards, he took revenge by killing him. Olaf was rescued from slavery when he was recognized, years later, in an Estonian slave market by his maternal uncle Sigurd. This almost mythic sequence of events brought Olaf to Holmgard (Novgorod), his destination many years before. He served King Valdemar as retainer and commander of his troops with great distinction until Valdemar became suspicious and envious of this young man with royal pretensions.

Olaf took to life as a successful Viking in the Baltic Sea. In 982, he married Geira, daughter of Burizleif, king of Vindland. He remained in Vindland for the next few years, continuing to raid and participating in the emperor Otto III's invasion of Denmark. With a secure base in Vindland, Olaf was becoming a serious player in Baltic affairs. After the death of his wife in the mid-980s, Olaf began plundering farther afield in the North Sea and in the Hebrides. In England, he married Gyda, sister of Olaf Cuaran, king of Dublin. Both his marriages were to powerful women who must have brought considerable wealth and influence to the partnerships.

The *Anglo-Saxon Chronicle* states that Olaf's fleet was responsible for the defeat of the Anglo-Saxons at the battle of Maldon in 991. Powerfully influenced by the prophecy of a seer, he was baptized in 994. He was an enthusiastic convert: *The Saga of the Orkney Islanders* (*Orkneyinga saga*) tells of his deception and forcible conversion of the earl of Orkney. He is also credited with baptizing Leif Eiriksson and sending him to convert Greenland.

Norway was ruled at that time by Earl Hakon, the nominal vassal of the king of Denmark. Hakon had adopted Christianity when he and Harald Bluetooth were defeated by the emperor Otto III. Before long, he had lapsed into his former paganism and had become a thoroughly unpopular ruler. In 995, hearing of a possible claimant to the throne in England, he sent two envoys to trick Olaf into returning to Norway, but the envoys informed Olaf of Hakon's plot so that he arrived in Norway forewarned and immediately had himself acclaimed as king. Hakon's resistance crumbled and he was run to ground in a pig-sty, where he was murdered by his sole companion, a slave called Kark. Kark presented the head to Olaf, but, instead of the expected reward, he was himself beheaded. Olaf went on to establish his capital at Trondheim.

Olaf spent a considerable part of his short reign in the forcible, often brutal, conversion of Norway. He executed pagan sorcerers, drowning some and burning others. He inflicted hideous torments on those who resisted conversion. Conversion was as much a matter of asserting political dominance as it was of spreading the faith. It was said that Greenland, the Shetlands, the Faeroes, Iceland, and Orkney became officially Christian at his bidding, though there is doubt about this.

Olaf is said to have provoked the hostility of Svein Forkbeard, king of Denmark, by marrying his sister, Thyre, without permission. Thyre was already married to Burizleif, king of Vindland, Olaf's former father-in-law. The saga-literature regards this insult as the prime cause of the alliance against Olaf forged by Svein Forkbeard, Olaf king of Sweden, and Earl Eirik, the son of the murdered earl Hakon of Norway. The allies caught Olaf at Svold in Oresund on his way back from a successful expedition to claim Thyre's property from Burizleif in Vindland. After a heroic resistance, Olaf was defeated, fighting splendidly on his flagship, the *Long Serpent*. Snorri's account of the battle is particularly gripping. Olaf, it is said, managed to swim away and was sighted several times over the following years.

A more probable cause of the alliance against Olaf was his success in subduing Norway and imposing his moral authority on the Atlantic colonies that were to form the Norwegian empire. His final voyage to Vindland with a large fleet was perhaps regarded as an aggressive assertion of regional ambitions. His ambition for Sweden was already clear, and, with his long-standing influence in Vindland, may be seen a desire to transform the Baltic into a Norwegian lake. Olaf had a long and successful military career as a Viking and soldier. Saint Olaf (Olaf Haraldsson) was later to make a similar leap from Viking to king in Norway.

Beneath the swashbuckling epic of Viking raids and miraculous escapes, there is the sense of a steely ambition. Olaf's moral and political subjugation of Norway may be seen as expressing the same ruthless will to power.

HARALD HARDRADI, KING OF NORWAY (R. 1047–66): THE "HARD-RULER"

The sagas extend Harald's name by the addition of *harðráði,* which may be translated as "hard or cruel ruler." According to *Fagrskinna* and *Heimskringla,* his claim to the throne of Norway was based on his (dubious) descent from King Harald Finehair.

Harald Hardradi Sigurdarson was the half-brother of King Olaf Haraldsson (Saint Olaf, 995–1030), who died at the battle of Stiklestad. Harald was wounded in the battle but escaped to Holmgard (Novgorod), where he received the favor of King Jarizleif. After several years of military service with Jarizleif, he took the Norseman's familiar road east to Byzantium.

According to *Heimskringla*, Harald joined and later commanded the Varangian Guard, the emperor's bodyguard, which was recruited in that period mainly among Norsemen. Harald's military successes humiliated his Byzantine colleague, Gyrges. On one occasion, Harald used birds carrying fire to destroy a city he was besieging. His subsequent career in the Middle East was an unbroken series of triumphs. After accumulating a vast fortune, he wished to return home, but the empress Zoe had designs on him and persuaded the emperor not to let him go. With his customary brilliance, Harald escaped (after putting out the emperor's eyes), returned to Holmgard, and married Ellisif, the daughter of Jarizleif. Snorri's account has a liberal element of the fantastic and is hardly a reliable authority on Harald's career in Byzantium.

A more sober view of Harald's eastern adventures is offered by the Byzantine writer Kekaumenos. According to Kekaumenos, Harald arrived in Byzantium with a retinue of five hundred, fought with some distinction on behalf of the emperor in Sicily and Bulgaria, and was rewarded with the ranks of *manglavites* (member of a corps of the imperial guard) and *spatharocandidatos* (about the middle of the Byzantine hierarchy). Kekaumenos confirms that Harald had difficulty leaving Byzantium and that he escaped secretly.

After marriage to Ellisif, Harald returned to Scandinavia, laden with treasure and honors. His nephew Magnus the Good (1024–47), an illegitimate son of Saint Olaf, occupied the thrones of Norway and Denmark. Magnus is reputed to have destroyed the Jomsvikings and had ambitions to restore the North Sea empire of Cnut the Great. Harald first tried to persuade Svein Ulfsson (ca 1019–74), claimant to the Danish throne, to support an attempt to dethrone his nephew. Magnus saw the wisdom of sharing his kingdom with Harald, and the two ruled together peaceably until the unexpected death of Magnus the Good two years later. Magnus had ruled both Denmark and Norway, but Harald was never able to suppress the attempts of Svein Ulfsson to take the Danish throne. In the long run, Harald gave up his claim to Denmark.

As was the case with Olaf Tryggvason, Norway was insufficient for Harald's ambition. In 1066, he seized the chance to invade England, which was in a state of unrest after the death of Edward the Confessor and the succession of Harold Godwinsson. Harold Godwinsson's brother, Tostig, had claims of his own and persuaded Harald of Norway to invade England on his behalf. Initially, the invasion went well. Harald defeated the English forces sent against him and received the surrender of the city of York. He became over-confident, however, and was taken completely by surprise when Harold Godwinsson appeared before him after a remarkable forced march. The Norwegians were completely unprepared. Part of their army was still aboard ship, and those ashore were not wearing their armor as it was a warm day. At the battle of Stamford Bridge, Harald and a large number of his men perished. Harald's defeat ended the last serious Norwegian attempt to invade and hold England.

A few days later, Duke William of Normandy, descendant of another Norseman, invaded England. Harold Godwinsson died fighting at Hastings (14 October 1066).

EIRIK THE RED AND LEIF EIRIKSSON: EXPLORERS OF THE NORTH ATLANTIC (CA 980–1000)

Eirik and his family won fame through the discovery, exploration, and settlement of new lands in the North Atlantic, especially Greenland and Vínland. The story of Eirik and his family is narrated in two thirteenth-century sagas— *Eirik the Red's Saga* [ES] and *Saga of the Greenlanders* [GS], as well as two Icelandic historical texts, *The Book of the Icelanders* (*Íslendingabók*) and *The Book of Settlements* (*Landnámabók*).

Eirik and his father Thorvald were outlawed from Jaeren in west Norway for some killings. They emigrated to Iceland, where they settled at Drangar in the Westfjords. After the death of Eirik's father, Eirik married a local woman, Thjodhild, and the couple moved to a new farm at Eiriksstadir. Eirik had a propensity for trouble and soon became involved in further disputes and killings that led first to his banishment from Haukdale and ultimately to his outlawry from Iceland.

Unable to return to Norway, Eirik decided to search for new lands west of Iceland that had been sighted earlier by Gunnbjorn Ulfsson, who had been blown off course while sailing to Iceland. Sailing from the Snaefellsnes peninsula, Eirik was successful in his quest and spent three years reconnoitering the fjords and coastline on the southwestern tip of the new land. *ES* relates how Eirik called this place Greenland because "people would be much more eager to go there if the place had an attractive name." Although Eirik's choice of name has often been described as optimistic at best (if not a downright medieval real-estate scam), it is worthwhile remembering that, for land-hungry Scandinavians, the southwestern tip of Greenland, with its deeply indented fjords, offered an attractive environment and abundant natural resources.

After three years' reconnaissance, Eirik returned to Iceland, where he spent a winter and then departed to settle in Greenland. Twenty-five ships are said to have sailed from Iceland, but only 14 arrived, the remainder either driven back or destroyed in rough seas. The settlement of Greenland is placed in the mid-980s (985/86) by twelfth- and thirteenth-century Icelandic historical texts.

PHOTO 3.1   Brattahlid, Greenland. Eirik the Red's Brattahlid, modern Qassiarsuk, on the western side of Eriksfjord (Tunulliarfik Fjord), Greenland, as it appears today. An important site throughout the history of Norse Greenland, many of the ruins here postdate Eirik's late tenth-century settlement. Remains of a later medieval church and churchyard are visible near the center of the photograph. (Photo by R.A. McDonald)

In Greenland, Eirik had selected for himself a farm on prime pastureland: this was called *Brattahlið* ("Steep Slope"; modern Qassiarsuk), situated on inner Eiriksfjord. *Landnámabók* and *GS* describe the manner in which other settlers took land in the region, establishing the core of what came to be known as the Eastern and Western Settlements, eventually comprising some six hundred Norse farms scattered along the fjords of south Greenland. Other uninhabited parts of Greenland were exploited for their abundant natural resources; especially significant were the Northern Hunting Grounds where narwhal, walrus, and polar bears were taken. The delightful *Story of Audun from the Westfjords* (*Auðunar þáttr vestfirzka*) tells how an Icelander goes to Greenland, where he buys a polar bear with the intention of giving it to the king of Denmark, which he eventually succeeds in doing.

In Greenland, Eirik gained prestige as the first settler of a new land. He was "held in the highest esteem, and everyone deferred to his authority." The farm at Brattahlið became the site of a local assembly as well as one of the first churches in Greenland when Eirik's wife Thjodhild converted to Christianity. Eirik himself proved reluctant to convert, however, and *ES* remarks that, after her conversion, Thjodhild refused to sleep with Eirik. Eirik and Thjodhild had three sons, Leif, Thorvald, and Thorstein, and a daughter, Freydis. The exact date of Eirik's death is unknown but is believed to have been around the year 1000.

The first generation of the Greenland colony coincided with the discovery of new lands even farther west, and Eirik's family were pioneers in the exploration and exploitation of these lands. *ES* and *GS* have slightly different stories to tell when it comes to the voyages to these lands, but while they may disagree on who it was that first sighted these lands, they reveal that Eirik's family—Leif, Thorvald, Thorstein, and Freydis—all undertook expeditions there. *GS* tells how Leif named the lands according to the resources to be found there: Helluland (Slab-Rock Land), Markland (Forest Land), and Vínland (Wine Land). Leif's brother Thorvald is said to have been slain in a hostile encounter with natives in the region, and his sister Freydis undertook a commercial venture during which she had her business partners murdered. In general, exploitation of resources rather than settlement was the principal goal of these voyages, although *GS* says that on one voyage Thorfinn Karlsefni and his wife Gudrid (see below) took livestock and intended to settle if they could. One facet of the saga accounts that has been emphasized by scholars is the manner in which Leif retained strict control of the temporary structures (*buðir*, booths) that he erected in Vínland, suggesting that control of resources was a prime consideration.

The region described as Vínland in the sagas was located on the eastern seaboard of North America, although its precise location has been the subject of considerable debate. Some modern scholars situate it in the Gulf of St. Lawrence region. Whatever the case, the discovery of the remains of three Norse longhouses and a smithy at L'Anse aux Meadows in Newfoundland in the early 1960s corroborated the saga accounts of voyages across the North Atlantic. Although these voyages to North America occupy only a brief moment in the Viking Age, they are testament to the seafaring skills of the Norse and mark the first contact between Europe and the Americas.

BOX 3.1   *Bjarni Herjolfsson: The First European to Sight North America?*

Although credit for the discovery of North America is often given to Leif Eiriksson, *GS* relates how a merchant named Bjarni Herjolfsson, en route to visit his father in Greenland from Iceland, was blown off course and sighted new lands to the west of his intended destination. Bjarni and his men sailed past flat, wooded land, hilly forested land, and a mountainous land covered by glaciers, but Bjarni refused to explore them, preferring instead to sail back to Greenland. *GS* relates that Bjarni was thought rather incurious and was criticized for his decision, and it was left to Leif Eiriksson to purchase Bjarni's vessel and retrace his steps to the new lands.

GUDRID THORBJARNARDAUGHTER (FL. CA 1000): A FAR-TRAVELED VIKING WOMAN

Gudrid Thorbjarnardaughter was one of the most widely traveled women of the Viking Age. She outlived three husbands, participated in the Viking expansion westward to Greenland and Vínland, and witnessed the conversion of the Icelanders and Greenlanders to Christianity.

Most of what is known about Gudrid's life is related in two thirteenth-century sagas, *ES* and *GS*, which show fewer signs than some sagas of having been altered from their oral antecedents. Nonetheless, they cannot be taken as trustworthy historical documents. Genealogies at the end of the sagas suggest they were composed for Gudrid's descendants. Weaving together the saga accounts allows Gudrid's life to be reconstructed.

Gudrid, described as a strikingly attractive woman, was the daughter of Thorbjorn Vifilsson, a prosperous farmer at Laugarbrekka in the Snaefellesness peninsula in Iceland. When Thorbjorn's economic situation began to deteriorate, he decided to emigrate with his family to the new colony in Greenland. During their first winter in Greenland, a pagan seeress visited the farm where Gudrid and her family were staying. Gudrid initially resisted participating in a pagan chanting ritual, "because I am a Christian woman," but eventually relented; *ES* says that "Gudrid spoke the chant so well and so beautifully that people there said they had never heard anyone recite it in a fairer voice." The episode represents one of the most detailed of all saga depictions of a pagan ritual (*seiðr*), including a remarkable description of the pagan seeress. The passage also highlights the religious transformation as the old gods gave way to Christ; in fact, the conflict between the old and new religions constitutes a prominent theme in *ES* and *GS*.

Gudrid's first husband was a Norwegian named Thorir, about whom little is known beyond the fact that he was one of those rescued from a shipwreck by Leif Eiriksson. In Greenland, Gudrid married again, taking as her second husband Thorstein Eiriksson. His father was the legendary Eirik the Red (see above), founder of the Greenland colony and an old friend of Gudrid's father, so Gudrid entered the ranks of Greenland's foremost family. Thorstein fell ill and died soon after, however, and Gudrid went to live as a widow with Eirik at

PHOTO 3.2   Statue of Gudrid at Laugarbrekka, Iceland, where she is said to have been born. Her son Snorri is also depicted. Statue by the Icelandic sculptor Ásmundur Sveinsson (1893–1982). (Photo by R.A. McDonald)

Brattahlid. While staying at Brattahlid she met and married her third husband, a merchant of good repute named Thorfinn Karlsefni, whose epithet means "makings of a man."

Gudrid's arrival in Greenland coincided with the westward voyages of exploration to the newly discovered region of Vínland in the years around 1000. Both sagas remark that people in Greenland were talking about these new lands at the time, and Gudrid participated in several voyages. *ES* says that Gudrid accompanied her second husband Thorstein Eiriksson on an abortive expedition that spent a summer being tossed about at sea before returning to Greenland. On another voyage Karlsefni and Gudrid took livestock with them and intended to settle. They spent several years in the region, gathering resources and trading with the natives (whom the Norse called Skraelings), and Gudrid gave birth to a son named Snorri, who was thus the first European born in North America.

Relations between the Norse and the natives in Vínland grew strained, however, and Karlsefni returned to Greenland in a ship laden with the produce of the land—grapevines, berries, and skins. From Greenland, Karlsefni made a trading voyage to Norway, and afterwards he, Gudrid, and Snorri settled at Skagafjord in northern Iceland. *GS* relates how, after the death of her husband and the marriage of her son, "Gudrid left Iceland and traveled on a pilgrimage to Rome. On her return, she stayed with Snorri who by then had built a church at Glaumbaer. Afterwards, Gudrid became a nun and anchoress, and remained there until she died...." Recent archaeological excavations at Glaumbaer may have uncovered the farm where Gudrid and Snorri lived. A statue at Laugarbrekka in the Snaefellesness peninsula in Iceland (see photo 3.2) commemorates the accomplishments of this remarkable woman of the Viking Age.

UNN THE DEEP-MINDED (FL. CA 900): UNPARALLELED AMONG WOMEN

Unn the Deep-Minded plays an unusual role for a woman in the sagas of Icelanders. The writer of *The Saga of the People of Laxardale* calls her achievements unparalleled among women; one might add that few men could equal her success either. The settlement of Iceland is presented in the sagas of Icelanders as an enterprise carried out largely by well-born Norwegian males, upholding their sturdy independence against the tyranny of Harald Finehair. Several Icelandic families could trace their lineage to Norwegian nobility, or even royalty. It is not hard to see why the foundation myth took the form that it did.

This homogenous foundation myth obscures the role of women in the process and ignores the arrival of migrants from areas in which the Norse lived side by side with Gaels. In one way, at least, Unn conformed to the foundation myth: she was Norwegian in origin. She was the daughter of Ketil Flatnose, who held the noble rank of *hersir* in Norway. Ketil's refusal to accept the suzerainty of Harald Finehair caused him to abandon his Norwegian property and move with most of his dependents to the Norse settlements in the Scottish islands; both his sons migrated to Iceland instead. In Scotland, Unn married Olaf the White, ruler of the Viking kingdom of Dublin. Their son, Thorstein the Red, campaigned successfully in Scotland and was recognized as ruler of half the country, until the Scots treacherously murdered him.

Unn was in Caithness when her son died. Her husband and her father were both already dead, so Unn was left to look after herself, the daughters of Thorstein the Red, and her entire household. She saw no future for herself in Caithness, so she had a ship built secretly and escaped in it with her family and household. She headed for Iceland, but, on the way, stopped at Orkney and the Faeroes (both of them Norse colonies by this time), where she married two of Thorstein's daughters into the most prominent families of both places. Her journey northward had the air of a royal progress.

In Iceland, she carved out an immense land take for herself, in the Breidafjord area of western Iceland. She rewarded her loyal followers with property. We last see her celebrating the marriage of Thorstein the Red's son, Olaf, into a distinguished Icelandic family.

Quite apart from the feat of arranging a clandestine departure from Scotland, Unn played the role usually reserved for men in the Icelandic foundation myth as it is represented in the sagas. She acquired her own land take, which was comparable to those in the male-dominated landscape of the Icelandic settlement. She acted as a male head of household would: freeing slaves, distributing land, and marrying off her grandchildren.

Also, Unn is unusual among the settlers because of her Christianity and because she came from Scotland, rather than directly from Norway. There are several Gaelic names among the members of her household, and several important families in her land take were descended from these Gaelic migrants, many of whom were slaves when they arrived in Iceland. She reminds us of the important Celtic element in the colonization of Iceland and calls the customary settlement myth into question. She is the first of a series of strong women in *The Saga of the People of Laxardale*.

Unn was Christian, and so, probably, were those who accompanied her. In the light of this, how should we regard the assumption that everyone eventually blended into the pagan background? Could it be that the change of custom (conversion) was not as sudden as the sources affirm? Had the ground already been prepared? After all, Christianity cannot have seemed strange to the pillagers of western Europe, many of whom accepted the ritual known as prime-signing to legitimize their relations with Christian Europeans. Finally, several of the settlers of Greenland came from the west of Iceland, including Eirik the Red, according to Ari Thorgilsson. The apparent ease of Greenland's conversion may have some connection with this.

SVEIN ASLEIFARSON (D. CA 1171): THE LAST VIKING?

Svein Asleifarson is one of the most colorful and memorable characters in *The Saga of the Orkney Islanders* (*Orkneyinga saga*), a saga-history of the rulers of Orkney and Shetland between about 900 and 1200, composed in Iceland at the beginning of the thirteenth century. Svein's remarkable career, woven through some 40 chapters of the saga, embodies the complexities and contradictions of the Viking Age and in some ways symbolizes its end; he has been described both as "the Ultimate Viking" and "the Last Viking."

Farmer, fisher, pirate, warrior, chieftain, landlord, and confidant of earls and kings, Svein was the son of Olaf Hrolfsson, an Orkney chieftain, and Asleif, "a woman of good birth, great intelligence, and strong character." The early death of his father and his mother's strong character meant that he was known by the matronymic Asleifarsson. His early appearances in the saga interweave his blood feud against the slayers of his father with political intrigues that involved him in the dynamic rise and fall of several Orkney earls, in the course of which Svein slew a number of rivals. In one memorable episode, Svein burned Frakokk Moddansdaughter in her house in revenge for the killing of Svein's father.

The saga also tells of Svein's raiding in the Hebrides, the Isle of Man, Wales, and Ireland, and includes a famous description of his Viking lifestyle:

> At that time, it was Svein's custom to spend his winters at home in Gairsay, where he always kept eighty men around him at his own expense. His drinking hall was so large that there was nothing to equal it in the Orkneys. Svein was always very busy in the spring; he had a great quantity of seed planted, attending to much of the work himself. Every spring, when the planting was over, he went on a Viking expedition, raiding in the Hebrides and Ireland. He called this his spring-raid. He returned home after midsummer and stayed at home until the fields were harvested and the grain was stored. Then he went on another Viking trip and did not return until the first month of winter was over. He called this his autumn-raid. (Ch. 105)

On one occasion, Svein embarked upon a Viking trip to the Hebrides and Irish Sea with five ships, during which he robbed two English merchant vessels of everything they had, including mead, wine, and valuable English broadcloth, leaving the crews with only the clothes on their backs. The plundered textiles were stitched to the front of the ships' sails so that these seemed to be woven of precious fabric; because of this, the saga writer says, they named this expedition "the broad-cloth Viking trip."

Appropriately enough, Svein met his end on a plundering expedition in the Irish Sea, in the course of which he and his men were ambushed and slain in an attack upon Dublin. Scholars have linked his death to an attempt by allied Irish and Norse forces to liberate Dublin from the English, who had captured it in 1170. Irish annals record Orcadian raiders in the Irish Sea in 1170 and 1171, although Svein is not explicitly said to have been among them.

Svein's life, though undoubtedly embellished by the saga-author, nevertheless sheds light on many aspects of the late Norse world, from the ruthlessness of the feud and contemporary politics to the role of farming, fishing, and piracy in the economy. His reputation was enormous, and the author remarked of him that, "...except for men of higher rank than himself, he was the most outstanding of all the men in the Westlands, either past or present." Even to the saga-writer, however, Svein's death marked the end of an era. The saga relates how, following Svein's death, his sons, Olaf and Andres, set up partition walls in the great drinking hall their father had built on Gairsay. This represents the end of the saga as it was originally written, and serves as a symbol of the end of the Viking Age. The world was changing, and Svein has a legitimate claim to be regarded as the "last Viking."

CHAPTER FOUR

HOW DO WE KNOW ABOUT THE VIKINGS?

Viking studies involves many disciplines, such as history, archaeology, linguistics, and genetics. This chapter is concerned with the documentary evidence for the Norsemen in the Viking Age. It offers an overview of the variety of the documentary material as well as some basic tenets of source criticism applicable to that material.

SCANDINAVIAN SOURCES

Surviving documentary material from the Norsemen in the Viking Age is rare. The Vikings were not, however, completely illiterate on the eve of their expansion. Like other Germanic peoples, they possessed a runic alphabet called the *futhark*, which was well suited to carving short inscriptions on stone, wood, bone or metal to indicate owners' or makers' marks, memorials, boundary markers, and graffiti. Runes were never used for long narrative, and their study represents a branch of philology known as runology, a highly specialized discipline. Around six thousand runic inscriptions are known, unevenly distributed around the Viking world; about half of these are on runestones, many of them in Sweden. Runic inscriptions can be used as historical documents, and scholars have investigated such diverse topics as land ownership, inheritance, wealth, social ranks, women's roles and status, and the impact of Christianity. Most, however, date from the late Viking Age, and few are earlier than the mid-tenth century. Runic inscriptions are important evidence for the Vikings and their age, but their usefulness is limited.

Few written documents survive from Scandinavia before the eleventh century because the Scandinavians did not adopt the Roman alphabet until their conversion to Christianity. But it is only from about the middle of the tenth century that Christianity took firm root among the Scandinavians. It is, therefore, really only from the eleventh century that native Scandinavian written sources began to multiply, and they did not become abundant until the thirteenth, after the Viking Age had ended.

The Vikings have left a substantial and remarkable literature in both prose and poetry. The problem is that none of this material comes to us directly from the Viking Age, and it presents serious interpretative problems. For this reason, the corpus of poetic and saga material is considered separately below.

BOX 4.1 ***A Runic Inscription***

The *futhark* was known throughout the Germanic world and is probably based on North Italian alphabets. It is named after the initial sound of the first six rune-names F, U, Th, A, R, and K. Scandinavian inscriptions use either the Elder or Younger Futhark. The Elder Futhark is found on Germanic inscriptions from the second century CE until the eighth century, while the Younger Futhark was used in Scandinavia from ca 800 onward. The inscription below exemplifies the Younger Futhark:

ᚠᚢᚦᚬᚱᚴ ᚼᚾᛁᛅᛋ ᛏᛒᛘᛚᛦ
f u th a r k h n i a s t b m l r

Runes were often used in monumental inscriptions or as ownership marks, and they were also regarded as possessing magical properties. They were rarely employed to produce texts of a considerable length. Christianization and the arrival of the manuscript age in Scandinavia were accompanied by the introduction of the Latin alphabet even when the language of the text was vernacular. Both Old Norse and Anglo-Saxon retained the use of the rune *thorn* (i.e., Þ).

Harald Bluetooth's Memorial to his Parents at Jelling (see photo 2.3 and box 2.2)

SIDE A

ᚼᛅᚱᛅᛁᛏᚱ : ᚴᚢᛏᚢᚴᛦ : ᛒᛅᚦ : ᚴᛅᚢᚱᚢᛅ
ᚴᚢᛒᛚ : ᚦᛅᚢᛋᛁ : ᛏᚡᛏ : ᚴᚢᚱᛘ ᚡᛅᚦᚢᚱ ᛋᛁᚾ
ᛏᚢᚡ ᛏᚡᛏ : ᚦᛂᚢᚱᚢᛁ : ᛁᚢᚦᚢᚱ : ᛋᛁᛏᛏ : ᛋᛏ
ᚼᛅᚱᛅᛁᛏᚱ : ᛁᛏᛋ : ᛋᛂᛅ • ᚢᛏᛏ • ᛏᛅᛏᛁᛦᚢᚱᚡ

SIDE B

ᛅᛚᛅ ᛏᚢᚡ ᛏᚢᚱᚢᛁᛅᚡ

SIDE C

ᛏᚢᚡ ᛏᛏᛁ (ᚡᛅᚱᚦᛁ) ᚡᚱᛁᛋᛏᚾᚡ

The following transcriptions of the runes above are drawn from the Scandinavian Runic-text Database at the University of Uppsala. The entire database is accessible at http://www.nordiska.uu.se/forskn/samnord.htm.

Literal:

SIDE A

  haraltr : kunukʀ : baþ : kaurua
  kubl : þausi : aft : kurm faþur sin
  auk aft : þourui : muþur : sina : sa
  haraltr (:) ias : soʀ ★ uan ★ tanmaurk

SIDE B

  ala ★ auk nuruiak

SIDE C

  (★) auk t(a)ni (k)(a)(r)(þ)(i) kristno

Old West Norse:

  Haraldr konungr bað gera
  kuml þessi ept Gorm, fǫður sinn,

ok ept Þyrvé, móður sína, sá
Haraldr er sér vann Danmǫrk
alla ok Norveg
ok dani gerði kristna.

Original Language:
SIDE A

Haraldr kunungR baþ gørwa
kumbl þøsi æft Gorm, faþur sin,
ok æft Þorwi, moþur sina, sa
Haraldr æs seR wan Danmork

SIDE B
alla ok Norwæg

SIDE C
ok dani gærþi kristna.

English:
SIDE A

King Haraldr ordered
this monument made in memory of Gormr, his father,
and in memory of Thyrvé, his mother;
that Haraldr who won for himself all of Denmark

SIDE B
and Norway

SIDE C
and made the Danes Christian.

OHTHERE AND WULFSTAN (CA 871–899)

Apart from runic inscriptions, perhaps the closest we are able to come to individuals who speak to us directly from the Viking Age are the ninth-century voyagers Ohthere and Wulfstan. Even their accounts come to us through at least one intermediary, however. Their narratives are interpolated in the ninth-century Anglo-Saxon translation of Paulus Orosius's *Historia Contra Paganos* and describe an account of sea-voyages along the coast of Norway and through the Baltic Sea. This brief document provides an unparalleled glimpse of the Scandinavia of the period, but it remains stubbornly silent about how and why it came into existence. The geographical and historical worth of the passage is inestimable, but problems raised by the text are even more intriguing. Ohthere was a Norwegian chieftain from Halogaland. His wealth consisted mainly of reindeer, but he traded, hunted, and explored as well. He tells of a journey around the North Cape into the White Sea, and of another, south along the coast of Norway to the great trading port of Hedeby in Denmark. His dealings with the Sami, his whale hunting, the details of his farming, and the navigational information he presents are fascinating.

The opening words of the passage are, however, fraught with possibilities: "Ohthere told his lord, King Alfred...." This opening resembles the record of a conversation in which an intelligent questioner extracts detailed information about Ohthere's way of life. Indeed, it is easy to supply the missing questions to which Ohthere's words are the answers. The questioner appears to be Alfred the Great, king of the West Saxons (r. 871–899). But why would the pagan Ohthere regard Alfred as *his* lord? Were the two able to understand one another? If so, what language did they use? Were their languages mutually comprehensible? What was Ohthere doing in Alfred's presence? In what circumstances would a conversation such as this have taken place? Were the walrus tusks mentioned in the passage gifts to Alfred from Ohthere? The wonders of the north are here, but the commonplaces of how the text came into existence, and the cultural milieu from which it arose, remain obscure. Documents may conceal as much as they reveal to us, and they certainly do not speak for themselves.

The report of Wulfstan's sea-voyage through the Baltic begins in Hedeby, where Ohthere's ends. Beyond that, there is no relationship, and few similarities, between the two narratives. Wulfstan's name is Anglo-Saxon, and his narrative is radically different from Ohthere's, which has the coherence of actual voyages. Wulfstan's voyage, on the other hand, is part navigational guide, part geographical survey, and part ethnographical study. The name "Wulfstan" appears only near the beginning, and the presence of a personal narrator is hardly necessary to the rather academic discussion of the geography and ethnography of the region. Indeed, Wulfstan sets off from Hedeby to Truso, but he never actually arrives there.

The presence of such different texts in the same brief interpolation disguises the widely different cultural motives behind their creation, a difference not always recognized as clearly as it might.

BOX 4.2   *The Northmen in Their Own Words:* **The Voyage of Ohthere**

Source: trans. A.A. Somerville, from *Ohthere's Voyages,* ed. Janet Bately and Anton Eglert, *Maritime Culture of the North,* volume 1 (Roskilde: The Viking Ship Museum, 2007), pp. 44–47.

Ohthere told his lord, King Alfred, that he lived farther north than any other Norwegian. He said that he lived to the north of the country beside the West Sea. He said the land stretches a long way north from there, however, though it is completely unpopulated except for a few places here and there, where Sami live, hunting in winter and fishing by the sea in summer.

He said that on one occasion he wanted to find out how far north the land stretched, and whether anyone lived to the north of the wilderness area. So, he sailed north close to the coastline. For three days, he kept the wilderness to his starboard and the open sea to port. By then he was as far north as whalehunters ever go. After that, he kept traveling due north as far as he could sail in the next three days. Then the land turned to the east, or the sea curved into the land, he did not know which. But he did know that he waited there for a wind from the west-northwest and afterwards sailed east along the coast as far as he could sail in four days. Then he had to wait there for a north wind, because the land turned due south there, or the sea turned into the land, he did not know which. There a large river stretched into the land. They turned into the river, not daring to travel beyond it for fear of hostility, because the land on the other side of the river was thickly settled. Until now, he had not come across any populated land since leaving his own home; but all the way there was empty land to starboard except for fishermen, fowlers, and hunters, and they were all Sami and to port there was always the open sea. The Biarmians had settled their land thickly, but they [Ohthere and crew] dared not set foot there. The land of the Ter-Sami, however, was completely uninhabited except for hunters, fishermen, or fowlers.

The Biarmians told him many tales both about their own land and about the lands which lay around them, but he did not know how true these tales were because he did not see anything for himself. It seemed to him that the Sami and the Biarmians spoke much the same language.

In addition to exploring the land, he traveled there mainly for the walrus, because they have very fine bone in their teeth—they brought some teeth for the king—and their hide is very good for ships' ropes.

This whale is much smaller than other whales, being no more than seven ells long [an English ell is 1.14 m]. But, the best whale hunting is in his own land where the whales are 48 ells long, and the biggest 50 ells in length. He said that he and six other men killed 60 of them in two days.

He was a very well-to-do man, rich in the possessions which comprise their wealth, namely wild beasts. When he visited the king, he still had six hundred unsold animals. These animals are called reindeer. Six of them were decoy reindeer; these are highly prized by the Sami because they catch wild reindeer with them. He was one of the most prominent men in that land, yet he had no more than 20 cattle, 20 sheep, and 20 pigs, and the little that he plowed, he plowed with horses. Their wealth, however, consists mainly of the tribute paid to them by the Sami. This tribute consists of animal hides, bird feathers, whale bone, and ships' cables made from whale and seal skins. Each man pays according to his rank. The highest ranking must give 15 marten skins, five reindeer hides, a bear skin, 10 ambers of feathers, a bear or otter skin coat, and two ships' cables, each 60 ells long, one made from whale skin and the other from seal skin.

He said that the land of the Norwegians is very long and very narrow. All the land that can be grazed or ploughed lies beside the sea, and even that is very rocky in places. Above and to the east lie wild, mountainous waste-lands, stretching all along the length of the inhabited land. Sami inhabit the wasteland. The inhabited land is broadest to the east [that is, in the south of Norway] and the farther north it lies, the narrower it becomes. To the east, it can be 60 miles broad, or slightly broader, and in the middle, it can be 30 miles or broader. To the north, where it is narrowest, he said, it might be only three miles broad before becoming wasteland. In some places the wasteland is as wide as a man can cross in two weeks; in others, as wide as a man can cross in six days. Alongside the southern part of the land, on the other side of the wasteland, Sweden stretches up to the northern part of Norway, and adjacent to the northern part of Norway is Cwenland [land of the Sami]. Sometimes, the Sami harry the Norwegians across the waste land, and at other times the Norwegians raid them. There are huge freshwater lakes throughout the wastelands; the Sami carry their boats overland to the lakes and raid the Norwegians from there. They have very small, light boats.

Ohthere said that the district where he lived is called Halogaland and that no one lived to the north of him. In the south of that land is a port called Skiringssal [Kaupang]. He said that a man could not sail there in a month if he camped at night and had a favorable wind every day. And all the while, he must sail along the coast, and to his starboard, first there will be Ireland and then the islands between Ireland and this land [Britain]. Then Britain is to starboard until he comes to Skiringssal and, all the way, Norway lies to port. South of Skiringssal, a very large sea cuts deeply into the land; it is broader than anyone can see across. Jutland is opposite on the other side and then Sillende [central and southern Denmark]. The sea flows many hundreds of miles into the land. From Skiringssal, he said that he sailed for five days to the port called Hedeby which stands between the Wends, the Saxons, and the Angles and belongs to the Danes. When he sailed there from Skiringssal, Denmark was on his port side for three days and open sea on his starboard. Then, for two days before he came to Hedeby, Jutland, Sillende, and many islands lay to starboard—the Angles lived in these places before they came to this land [England]—and for these two days the islands that belong to Denmark lay to port.

VIKINGS IN EUROPEAN AND EASTERN SOURCES

Confronted with a lack of contemporary Scandinavian sources, scholars must turn elsewhere. Fortunately, the peoples with whom the Vikings interacted have left written records, including chronicles and annals, histories, letters, saints' lives, poetry, charters, sermons, official treatises on statecraft, diplomatic documents, and encyclopedias relating their encounters with Scandinavians across Europe and the Middle East. The use of this evidence, however, poses many challenges. It is written in many languages, including Irish, English, Latin, Russian, Greek, and Arabic. Apart from the difficulty of accurately translating these works, the manuscripts present many textual problems. These include considerations of whether we are dealing with an original manuscript or, more likely, a later copy, or even a copy of a copy; if the latter, has the text been altered, either deliberately or through mistakes of copying, over time? The purpose for which a text was written must be considered: often, scholars mine documents for historical information which they were not necessarily originally intended to provide. The practice of reading documents this way is sometimes called "reading against the grain," and it is important always to determine what the *original* purpose of a document was in order to assess its utility as a source. As it has been succinctly put, "... an author's intentions and prejudices and the directives of genre must be taken into consideration before his declarations of fact can be accepted" (Wolf 2004, xiii). Let us consider this principle in relation to several important sources of different types from Europe as an introductory exercise of some of the principles of source criticism.

Alcuin's Letter to King Athelred of Northumbria, 793

One of the most famous and oft-cited contemporary documents relating to an early raid by the Northmen is a letter written in Latin by the scholar Alcuin (ca 740–804) to the Northumbrian king Athelred. Alcuin's letter refers to the Viking attack on the monastery of Lindisfarne in the summer of 793 and explains it in terms of divine punishment. This document is one of our most important sources for the raid, as it was written shortly afterwards. The raid is mentioned in the *Anglo-Saxon Chronicle* for the year 793, but that text was not compiled until nearly a century later—and therefore technically does not constitute a primary source for the event.

Scholars have frequently quoted one passage of Alcuin's letter in particular:

> Lo, it is nearly 350 years that we and our fathers have inhabited this most lovely land, and never before has such terror appeared in Britain as we have now suffered from a pagan race, nor was it thought that such an inroad from the sea could be made. Behold, the Church of St. Cuthbert spattered with the blood of the priests of God, despoiled of its ornaments; a place more venerable than all in Britain is given as prey to pagan peoples. And where first, after the departure of Saint Paulinus from York, the Christian religion in our race took its rise, there misery and calamity have begun. Who does not fear this? Who does not lament this as if his country were captured? Foxes pillage the chosen vine, the heritage of the Lord has been given to the Gentiles; the holy festivity has been turned to mourning.

This appears to be a description by a well-informed contemporary of the stereotypical Viking raid: an unexpected assault from the sea, directed at a church, replete with violence, slain clergy, splattered blood, desecration, devastation, and the taking of plunder. But before Alcuin's account can be accepted at face value, the nature of the source needs to be examined.

First, Alcuin was not actually present at Lindisfarne (or indeed even in England) when the raid occurred; the letter was written from the Continent and is not, therefore, an eyewitness report. One important question, for which there is no firm answer, is how Alcuin received information on the raid. It is true that Alcuin spent the years from 790 to early 793 in Northumbria, but he is believed to have returned to the Frankish realm by the time the raid on Lindisfarne occurred. As subsequent letters demonstrate, Alcuin retained contacts with his native Northumbria; perhaps he received information from witnesses there. Moreover, Alcuin was connected with the Carolingian court, which was beginning to cope with increased Scandinavian activities in the North Sea and which had diplomatic and political dealings with Danish dynasts at the time. Alcuin was probably quite well informed on the Scandinavian homelands and peoples and on Scandinavian affairs in Britain and the Continent. Indeed, Alcuin was writing from within a Carolingian Empire that was increasingly embroiled in border wars with the Danes. This has led one writer to conclude that Alcuin's letters cannot be regarded as objective accounts, but as "arguments in a political and ideological conflict" that sought the conquest and conversion of the Scandinavians (Myhre 1993, 197).

Stylistic considerations are also important in assessing a source. Many of Alcuin's letters of the period are admonitory in nature and employ stylistic commonplaces in similar ways. To what extent did concerns of style and genre shape the content of the letter, which is one of a series written by Alcuin at the time? But even such admonitory letters could be adapted by the writer to particular circumstances and recipients, demonstrating individuality while conforming to a particular genre. Disentangling rhetoric and stylistic convention from hard historical fact is one of the challenges presented by the use of sources such as this.

One interesting aspect of Alcuin's letter is the extent to which it accurately represents the Scandinavians as a hitherto unknown presence in the waters of Britain and northern Europe. Alcuin wrote, "... never before has such terror appeared in Britain as we have now suffered from a pagan race, nor was it thought that such an inroad from the sea could be made...." But is this accurate? Were the Viking raids really as unexpected as Alcuin would have us believe? It is unlikely that Alcuin, with his close connections to the Carolingian court, was uninformed about Scandinavian peoples and affairs. Indeed, later in the letter, Alcuin includes the imitation of pagan fashions in his list of sins for which the Northumbrians were being punished by Viking raids: "Consider the dress, the way of wearing the hair, the luxurious habits of the princes and people. Look at your trimming of the beard and hair, in which you have wished to resemble the pagans. Are you not menaced by terror of them whose fashion you wished to follow?" The Vikings may not have been so unknown to Alcuin and the people of Northumbria after all, and the passage has become an important plank in the arguments of scholars who argue for considerable contact between Scandinavia and Britain in the eighth century and who effectively downplay the unexpected nature of Viking raiding.

The Anglo-Saxon Chronicle, *Late Ninth Century*

Chronicles and annals are among the most characteristic historical texts produced in the Middle Ages, although they are not the only ones. Typically comprising brief records of yearly events in chronological order that lack analysis
or interpretation, their origins lie in the need to calculate the correct date for
the celebration of Easter, the most important festival in the Christian ritual
year. Into the tables produced for this purpose important events were recorded,
their brevity determined by considerations of space between lines or the size of
the margins. A distinction is sometimes made between chronicles and literary
histories, though the lines can be blurred, just as the concepts of chronicles
and annals can also overlap. Most chronicles and annals were anonymously
produced in religious communities, and were written in Latin, although there
are exceptions. Scholars distinguish between "dead" chronicles, in which an
author retrospectively gathered material up to his own time without recording
further events, and "live" chronicles, in which subsequent events continued to
be added, so that the chronicle grew almost organically.

Many medieval chronicles and annals survive for the so-called Viking Age.
Some are well informed on contemporary events and cannot be ignored as
sources for the Viking period even if their perspective on the Northmen often
appears as that of the victim. One of the most detailed chronicle accounts of
the entire Viking period is the *Anglo-Saxon Chronicle*, which covers the history
of England from 60 BCE until 1154 CE and has been described as "the best
of all the chronicles for the Viking period" (Sawyer 1962, 13). Even a casual
glance at this text will suggest something of its significance for the study of the
Viking Age: there are accounts of the earliest Viking raids on Lindisfarne and
Jarrow in 793 and 794, as well as the famous encounter between Northmen
and a royal representative at Portland in 789; of increased Danish raiding from
835 and the first overwintering in England in 850/51; of the activities of the
infamous "Great Heathen Army" from its arrival in East Anglia in 865 to its
dispersal in 896. From 865 until the early tenth century—and then again from
980 until about 1019—the *Chronicle* is almost exclusively concerned with the
activities of the Vikings in England; it has been suggested that it may have been
compiled specifically to record the struggle of King Alfred and his descendants
with the raiders, and more than a touch of propaganda has been discerned in
the *Chronicle*'s account of these events.

Is all the information in the *Chronicle* of equal value? Assessing this important question requires some understanding of the nature of the *Chronicle* as
well as the circumstances of its compilation. To begin with, the *Anglo-Saxon
Chronicle* is not the title of a single document but refers collectively to a group

of nine manuscripts, none of which is the original copy, and which all demonstrate considerable local variation. The earliest surviving manuscript is MS A, the *Parker* or *Winchester Chronicle,* begun in Wessex during the late ninth century. This version begins at 60 BCE and ends with the year 1070. There were, of course, no Anglo-Saxons in 60 BCE; early material on the history of Roman Britain was inserted later. The last entries in any version of the *Chronicle* appear in MS E, the *Peterborough* or *Laud Chronicle,* which finishes with the year 1154. The *Chronicle* is noteworthy for being written in the vernacular rather than in Latin, the language in which contemporary chronicles were usually composed.

Scholars agree that the *Chronicle* originated in the south of England, probably in Wessex, in the late ninth century. It is often associated with Alfred, king of the West Saxons, and his revival of learning, but whether that is the case or not, it is thought that the compiler began writing in 892. Leaving aside the complicated textual history of the nine surviving versions of the *Chronicle,* it is important to understand the sources of information upon which the anonymous compiler drew. Did he have access to earlier records? And since he began writing only in the 890s, what value does the chronicle have for references to Viking activity before then?

Study of the ninth-century entries in the *Chronicle* has illuminated the means by which it was put together. The regular, yearly entries from 865 to 892 suggest that the compiler had a detailed knowledge of events in this period, and he has been regarded as a contemporary witness. But what of the period before 865? The earliest Viking raids occurred a century before the *Chronicle* began to be assembled, so can it be treated as an authoritative source for the first half of the ninth century? Here, it has been pointed out that the entries from 821 to 842–843 contrast strongly with those from 842–843 to 865: while there are annals for almost every year from 821 to 842–843, there are only a few entries between 843 and 865. This has been taken to indicate that the compiler drew on an earlier, possibly contemporary, set of annals for the years 821 to 842–843, but that after 842–843, down to 865, he was probably relying on memory.

Nor is it clear what sources underlie the account of the first Viking raid on Wessex in 789. What is noteworthy is the *Chronicle's* comment that "These were the first Danish ships to attack the land of the English people..."—an observation that clearly demonstrates the benefit of hindsight. Another indication of a change in source material is the fact that from the late 880s to the early 890s there is a change in the date from which the beginning of the year was reckoned in the *Chronicle.* What all of this means is that the value of the *Chronicle* varies depending upon which period is under scrutiny: its authority for the middle years of the ninth century, from 843 to 865, has been seen as less than for the years before or after, although even this does not mean that the annals between 843 and 865 have no value at all. As one scholar aptly summed it up, "The Alfredian chronicle itself can be compared with a Russian doll: it incorporates earlier annals which in their turn incorporated still earlier ones, and so on..." (Gransden 1974, 36).

The *Chronicle* is not without other limitations. One is that its very detail should not blind us to the fact that it is not a comprehensive record of Viking activities in England and that much Viking activity in England is unrecorded, forgotten, or downplayed (Dumville 2008). To take one example: consider the cryptic reference to Scandinavian settlement in Northumbria in 876, when the *Chronicle* relates that "Halfdan divided up the land of Northumbria; the raiders became tillers of the land as well." Halfdan was one of the leaders of the Great Army, but the entry raises far more questions than it answers. The *Chronicle* can, therefore, be woefully and frustratingly lacking in information on certain aspects of Viking activity, although it is always pertinent to bear in mind that what is omitted from a chronicle, if it can be known, may be as significant as what was included.

Regional analysis of the *Chronicle's* record of Viking activities highlights the point. Unsurprisingly, given its Wessex origin, the *Chronicle* is best informed about the lands south of the Thames and the West Country; indeed, the compiler sometimes demonstrates detailed knowledge of local topography. There is, however, much less detailed information about other parts of the country. We have at best a vague understanding of what was occurring in places that were beyond the chronicler's horizon and have left no records of their own (such as East Anglia or Essex, for instance). Even for Wessex, the *Chronicle's* account has gaps: a raid on Southampton in 842, for instance, is omitted in the *Chronicle* but was recorded by Nithard (d. 844), a contemporary continental writer. Other such gaps have been detected. For example, there is a notable lack of information in the *Chronicle* concerning Viking settlement in some areas, particularly the east and northwest. Lacking contemporary written evidence on the subject, our understanding thus hinges on other disciplines such as linguistics (through place-name studies), archaeology, and art history.

Another subject of debate is the *Chronicle's* mention of the number of ships in Viking fleets. Peter Sawyer (1962) was one of the first scholars to question this matter. He argued that, although small fleets are often numbered exactly, references to larger fleets—such as that of 851, said to have had 350 ships—should not be treated as accurate reports. Although neither Sawyer's analysis nor his conclusions concerning the size of ninth-century Viking fleets and armies have been universally accepted (Brooks 1979), his advice that all figures given in medieval chronicles must be approached with caution remains sound. The largest fleet recorded by a contemporary source is the 700 ships said by

Abbo to have undertaken the attack on Paris in 885–886; it is little wonder, then, that Abbo has been described as being "in a class of his own as an exaggerator" (Brooks 1979, 6).

The *Anglo-Saxon Chronicle* therefore has both advantages and disadvantages as a source for Viking activity. Although it is often well informed and can be astonishingly detailed, a sound understanding of the means by which it was created, the nature of the sources upon which it was based, and a critical approach to the information it contains are all necessary before its evidence can be accepted. Despite detailed passages, we should remember that much has been forgotten, omitted, or slanted.

The excerpt from the *Chronicle* presented below relates to the activities of the Great Army in England between 866 and 869. As noted above, this section of the *Chronicle* has the appearance of being a contemporary record. It serves to illustrate the form and nature of a medieval chronicle dealing with the Vikings, and also illuminates a number of important points relating to Viking activities in England in the second half of the ninth century.

BOX 4.3   *The* **Anglo-Saxon Chronicle** *on the Great Army in England, 866–869*

Source: trans. A.A. Somerville, from David Dumville and Simon Keynes, general eds., *The Anglo-Saxon Chronicle: A Collaborative Edition* (Cambridge: D.S. Brewer, 1983–), volume 7; MS E, ed. Susan Irvine (Cambridge: D.S. Brewer, 2004), pp. 46–53.

[The chronology of this section is based on a year that seems to have begun on 24 September; original scribal dates are included, but adjusted dates are provided in parentheses, following the edition by Swanton (2000). Chronological discrepancies are just one of many challenges in dealing with chronicles and annals.]

867 [866]. This year, the heathen army advanced from East Anglia across the mouth of the River Humber as far as York in Northumbria. The Northumbrians were seriously at odds with one another. They had recently overthrown their king, Osbriht, and had accepted as king, Ella, a man with no claim to the throne. However, late in the year they submitted again to Osbriht and then fought against the heathen army. They gathered an immense host and attacked the heathens at York. They penetrated the fortifications and some of them got inside. There was a huge slaughter among the Northumbrians, some inside the city and others outside. Both Northumbrian kings were killed. The survivors made peace with the heathen army....

868 [867]. In this year, the heathen army moved to Nottingham in Mercia and took up winter quarters there. King Burgred of Mercia and his council begged King Athelred of Wessex and his brother Alfred to help them in their fight against the great army. They led the West Saxon host into Mercia as far as Nottingham where they encountered the heathen army at the fortifications and laid siege to the city. However, there was no serious fighting, so the Mercians made peace with the army.

869. In this year, the heathen army returned to York and stayed there for a year.

870 [869]. In the course of this year, the Danish army crossed Mercia on its way to East Anglia where they took up winter quarters at Thetford. The king of East Anglia, Saint Edmund, fought them, but the Danes won the battle and killed the king. They overran the whole land and destroyed all the monasteries they came to. At that time, they stormed and burned Medeshamstede [Peterborough] where they killed the abbot and the monks. They destroyed everything they found there and reduced to nothing a place that had formerly been very prosperous....

BOX 4.4   *The Vikings in European Chronicles and Annals*

The preceding discussion has used the *Anglo-Saxon Chronicle* as an example, but it is by no means unique. Many other chronicles and annals from the early Middle Ages contain information on Viking activities. A comprehensive listing would require much more space than is available here, but some other examples include the following:

The Annals of Ulster, an important set of Irish annals that survives only in a late medieval copy but is based upon contemporary records. It is one of the most valuable Irish sources on the Viking Age.

The Annals of St. Bertin, produced in the 830s as a court chronicle under Louis the Pious (r. 814–840) and later continued away from court by Prudentius of Troyes and Hincmar of Rheims. They cover the years 830 to 882 and comprise the single most important source for the activities of the Vikings on the Continent.

The Annals of St-Vaast, written at that monastery near Corbie, are an important window into the late ninth century. The entries for this period are particularly concerned with the activities of the Northmen and recount the siege of Paris by the Vikings in 885–886.

The *Royal Frankish Annals* is a composite work that covers the period 741 to 829. It was written at the Frankish court and is an important source for the reign of Charlemagne (r. 768–814). It is regarded as an official court source and demonstrates detailed knowledge of contemporary events. Military activities are to the forefront, and the annals provide contemporary evidence of relations between the Carolingians and the Northmen; in later entries it is very well informed on Scandinavian affairs.

The *Russian Primary Chronicle* or *Tale of Bygone Years* is one of the most important sources relating to the Scandinavians in the east. It covers the period from about 850 to the early twelfth century, but it was compiled after the mid-eleventh century and the value of its information before about 1050 is debated. It draws on earlier documents, interweaving historical and legendary material, and its account of the "Calling of the Varangians" in 859–862 is hotly contested.

The Battle of Maldon and The Battle of Maldon: *Records of a Viking Raid*

For the year 991, the *Anglo-Saxon Chronicle* records a battle between an Anglo-Saxon ealdorman and a Viking raiding party near Maldon in Essex:

> In this year, Ipswich (in Essex) was ravaged; and very soon after that Aldorman [high-ranking nobleman] Brihtnoth was killed at Maldon. And in that year it was decided for the first time to pay the Danes tribute because of the terrible damage they did along the sea coast. That first tribute was ten thousand pounds [of silver]. Archbishop Sigeric argued in favour of this plan.

The encounter was remembered very differently in the Anglo-Saxon poem *The Battle of Maldon*, composed shortly after the battle. According to the poem, Brihtnoth had bottled up the Vikings on Northey Island in the Blackwater River. The island was linked to the mainland by a narrow causeway that was submerged at high tide. The causeway was controlled by Brihtnoth and his men. Had he chosen, he could have waited out the Vikings. Instead, he allowed them to cross to the mainland. Numbers on either side are uncertain. Brihtnoth's force was formed from the local levy (*fierde*) together with the professional soldiers of his *heorðwerod* (lit. hearth-host; bodyguard). The composition of the Viking force is not known, but it has been suggested that it was likely to have been more experienced and professional than most of Brihtnoth's host.

The poem attributes Brihtnoth's decision to fight to his *ofermōd*, usually interpreted as *pride*. The view that Brihtnoth's decision was unwise is supported by the fact that the Anglo-Saxon force immediately adopted a defensive formation when the Vikings crossed the causeway; this suggests that Birhtnoth's force was weak, because of either numbers or lack of professionalism among the levy. The Anglo-Saxon force was apparently destroyed; Brihtnoth's head was carried off as a trophy by the Vikings.

The poem transforms the defeat into a splendid display of Anglo-Saxon courage that breathes the spirit of Germanic heroic idealism. There is a spirited exchange of abuse between Brihtnoth and a Viking messenger. The poem singles out the cowardice of those who fled and gives lapidary expression to the heroism of those who stayed to fight and die beside Brihtnoth's body. Even a humble Anglo-Saxon churl, Dunnere, is given an opportunity to express his heroic loyalty. The most memorable speech is that of the old retainer Byrhtwold; W.H. Auden translates part of it as follows:

Hige sceal þe heardra, heorte þe cenre,
mod sceal þe mare, þe ure mægen lytlað.
— *The Battle of Maldon*, 11. 312–13

Heart and head shall be keener, mood the more
As our might lessens.
— W.H. Auden, "Ode"

Many have asked why Brihtnoth allowed what was probably an unequal contest to take place. Was pride the cause, as the poem suggests? Possibly Brihtnoth saw an opportunity to attempt to limit the damages inflicted by the raiders. Brihtnoth, however, was a very important figure in Anglo-Saxon political life and it may be that he saw national dimensions in this local skirmish. The *Chronicle* mentions the fate of Brihtnoth and (perhaps pointedly) goes on to associate another prominent political figure, Archbishop Sigeric, with the policy of appeasement adopted by the royal government. Is a judgment of the two men and their policies implied?

Olaf Tryggvason, the future king of Norway, was raiding in English waters that year, and some have suggested that he was involved in the battle. His presence might help explain Brihtnoth's anxiety to fight, but that is highly speculative. It is at least possible that part of his fleet was present. Brihtnoth's tomb is in Ely Cathedral.

Adam of Bremen: History of the Archbishops of Hamburg-Bremen, *ca 1075*

Another important source for early medieval Scandinavia is the *Gesta Hammaburgensis ecclesiae pontificum* (*History of the Archbishops of Hamburg-Bremen*) of Adam of Bremen. Adam was a German cleric who came to Bremen about 1066–67 and became a canon of the cathedral chapter there. His text is a history of the diocese and its archbishops, written ca 1072–75/76 and revised down to the early 1080s, when he probably died. Because the archbishops of Hamburg-Bremen were charged with the conversion of the neighboring peoples of the north, Adam was particularly interested in their manners and customs. The work consists of four books. In book four, *Descriptio insularum aquilonis* (Description of the Isles of the North), Adam discusses the northern lands, describing the Danes, Swedes, and Norwegians as well as the Baltic and the islands of the North Atlantic.

Adam's *History* comprises arguably the single most important foreign narrative for Scandinavian history before 1100 and represents an early systematic example of ethnographic writing. But the information it provides cannot be taken at face value. Though Adam was well informed, drew on a wide range of sources, and was personally acquainted with the Danish king Svein Estridsson (d. 1074), who was one of his informants, most of Adam's information was hearsay rather than first-hand experience. Significantly, he wrote not only from a Christian perspective, but also with the interests of the diocese of Hamburg-Bremen firmly in mind: his main purpose was not simply to describe the history of the see, but to support the authority of the archbishops of Hamburg-Bremen over the church in Scandinavia (Sawyer and Sawyer 1993, 222–23).

Adam's account of the "temple" at Uppsala in Sweden (Book IV, ch. 26–27) exemplifies the challenges inherent in using this text as a source. Adam describes how golden statues of three gods, Odin, Freyr, and Thor (said to be the mightiest of the gods), were housed in the temple, where sacrifices were presided over by priests. He also relates that every nine years people from all over Sweden attended a festival at which "of every living thing that is male, they offer nine heads, with the blood of which it is customary to placate gods of this sort. The bodies they hang in the sacred grove that adjoins the temple. Now this grove is so sacred in the eyes of the heathen that each and every tree in it is believed divine because of the death or putrefaction of the victims. Even dogs and horses hang there with men." Adam's source was "a Christian seventy-two years old" who had witnessed these things with his own eyes, and he concludes his account with the remark that "it is better to keep silent" about some of the incantations used in the ritual. We have a seemingly detailed and well-informed account of Norse worship in the eleventh century. But how reliable is it?

Almost every aspect of Adam's account of the temple at Uppsala may be called into question; it has been suggested that it is nothing more than a fiction designed to enhance the need for missionary activity in the north. Modern scholarship is divided over the role played by "temples" in pre-Christian Scandinavian religion—whether they were used at all and whether there is any evidence for such a structure at Uppsala. Adam's description of the "temple" may be nothing more than the superimposition of something familiar—a Christian church—upon pagan Norse religious practice, which he only imperfectly understood. Adam's claim that there was a distinct priestly caste in Old Norse religion is also questioned by scholars, who point instead to the religious role played by chieftains. Adam's account of a "national" festival assumes a degree of uniformity and organization, which is seen as unlikely. Adam may, consciously or unconsciously, have been influenced by eleventh-century Christianity, with its specialized priestly caste and centralized structure. Also, the description of Thor as the mightiest of the gods is at odds with information from Icelandic sources, in which Odin is commonly described as the greatest of the Norse deities. Finally, Adam's Christian perspective and disgust at the whole pagan enterprise are reflected in his reluctance to relate further details of Norse worship. It is thus possible to call into question nearly every part of Adam's account.

Such an approach might be too severe; identification of "bias" does not necessarily mean total rejection of a source. Recent geophysical surveys of Uppsala, for example, have detected the remains of what has been interpreted as a large feasting hall. When combined with other research that emphasizes the role of feasting halls as places where religious ritual occurred, it may be possible to make some sense of Adam's account after all: was his "temple" actually a feasting hall in which religious rituals were performed? Sacred groves and other natural locations were important in Norse religion: the place name Odense in Denmark, for instance, means "Odin's grove." And what of Adam's account of human and animal sacrifice? These practices, too, are known in Norse religion. One oft-cited example is the Muslim diplomat Ibn Fadlan's eye-witness account of the sacrifice of a slave girl to accompany her dead master to the otherworld when he encountered Rūs on the Volga in 922. However, Ibn Fadlan's account has been much debated and must be used with caution (see below). Meanwhile, archaeological sites such as the burial at Ballateare in the Isle of Man may further illuminate the practice of human sacrifice.

Debate about the veracity and value of Adam's account of the "temple" at Uppsala will continue, but this example highlights the careful scrutiny to which a source must be subjected before its evidence can be used.

ARABIC SOURCES ON THE VIKINGS

Arabic sources contain important information on the Vikings in Islamic Spain, the Mediterranean, Russia, and the Middle East. Depending on the geographical context, the Vikings are usually referred to as Magians (al-Majus) or Rūs (al-Rus) in these texts. These accounts are numerous, and it is not possible to examine them all in detail; see Montgomery (2008) for more details.

Unquestionably the most famous of these accounts is that of Ibn Fadlan, a diplomat who traveled from Baghdad to the king of the Volga Bhulgar in 921–922. His *Risala* or *Writings* includes, as part of the discussion of the various peoples encountered by the embassy, a description of a meeting with Rūs on the Volga and an eye-witness account of the funeral of one of their chieftains as well as references to religious practices. Whether these Rūs were Scandinavians is, however, hotly contested. Ibn Fadlan's account formed the basis for part of Michael Crichton's novel *Eaters of the Dead* as well as the Hollywood film *The Thirteenth Warrior* (1999), which was based on Crichton's novel.

Ibn al-Qutiyya (d. 977) lived in Córdoba and authored an historical work on the *History of the Conquest of Andalusia*, which dealt with the period from the Islamic conquest to the early tenth century. It contains an account of a Viking attack on Lisbon in 844 and its aftermath.

BOX 4.5   *The Vikings through Byzantine Eyes*

De Administrando Imperio is a Byzantine source containing detailed information on the voyages of the Rūs to Constantinople in the mid-tenth century. It was compiled and written between 948 and 952 by the Byzantine emperor Constantine VII Porphyrogenitus (r. 945–959) and was intended as a confidential manual of kingship for his son. It has been called the most important of the Byzantine sources concerned with the Rūs. Contained within its discussion of the neighbors of the Byzantine Empire is a detailed account (one of only two surviving) of the so-called Viking road to Byzantium—the network of waterways, lakes, and portages that led from Scandinavia to Byzantium (Constantinople); within this network the Dnieper and Volga Rivers were key arteries.

Another interesting Islamic account is found in the works of the thirteenth-century Valencian writer Ibn Dihya (d. 1235). It recounts a diplomatic mission to the north by the renowned Arab poet and diplomat al-Ghazal ("the Gazelle") at the behest of the emir Abd-ar-Rahman II (r. 822–852), ruler of al-Andalus (the region in the Iberian Peninsula under the control of the Arabs), and has been used as evidence for diplomatic contacts between Scandinavia and the Islamic world. It has, for instance, been suggested that the "great island (or peninsula) in the ocean" visited by al-Ghazal refers to either Ireland or Denmark, and that the Viking king visited by al-Ghazal was either the Hiberno-Norse king Turgeis (d. 845) or the Danish ruler Horic (d. 854). Unfortunately, recent scholarship is skeptical of the historical authenticity of the account (Pons-Sanz 2004). As one scholar puts it rather bluntly, the story "has nothing to commend it beyond the charms of its fancy" (Montgomery 2008, 561).

LATER MEDIEVAL ICELANDIC SOURCES

Despite the paucity of contemporary Scandinavian material, the Vikings have left a substantial and remarkable literature, in both prose and poetry, the bulk of it vernacular. The major problem is that none of this material comes to us directly from the Viking Age, surviving instead in later texts. This material must be used with caution when it is employed to shed light on the Viking Age. The best-known form of Icelandic literature is the saga.

"Saga" is the term for the extensive prose narratives produced in medieval Scandinavia, most often in Iceland. By definition *saga* (pl. *sögur*) is related to *segja*, "to say, tell, report," and its root meaning is something said, or narrated orally: a story. The earliest meaning is presumably an extensive utterance; the term also applies to written stories, whether originally oral or not.

Though the form of the saga varied little, subject matter was diverse. Best known are the sagas of Icelanders (*Íslendinga sögur*; formerly, family sagas). These recount the colonization and development of Iceland by largely Norwegian settlers. Their problematic historicity is discussed below. Kings' sagas (*konungasögur*) are royal biographies and exist in several collections. Bishops' sagas are biographies of early Icelandic bishops; these are of some value for the history of the early Icelandic church. Legendary sagas (*fornaldarsögur*) are set in the old world before the age of Icelandic settlement (ca 870), a world of trolls, giants, magic, and semi-historical kings. Contemporary sagas (*samtíðarsögur/samtímasögur*) recount the civil wars of the thirteenth century and are generally contemporary with their subject matter. Related to the saga is the short story (*þáttr*). There follows a discussion of each type of saga and its contribution to our knowledge of the Viking Age.

The Sagas of Icelanders / Íslendinga sögur

The events narrated in the sagas of Icelanders take place during the Saga Age (ca 870–ca 1030), from the foundation of Iceland until shortly after the conversion in the year 1000. These sagas, formerly known as family sagas, were written down much later, mainly in the thirteenth and fourteenth centuries.

Many sagas begin with a foundation narrative telling of the departure for Iceland of the founders of prominent Icelandic families. *The Saga of the People of Laxardale* (*Laxdæla saga*) opens with the departure of the *hersir* (chief, lord) Ketil Flatnose from Norway for Scotland. Too proud to submit to the ambitions of Harald Finehair, he chooses instead to give up his ancestral home in Norway. His daughter, Unn the Deep-Minded (see chapter 3), marries Olaf the White, king of Dublin. After the deaths of her father, son, and husband, she makes an almost royal progress across the sea from Scotland to Iceland. Many sagas have similar foundation stories in which honorable or noble (even royal) Norwegians seek independence overseas rather than live in shame at home.

As part of their foundation stories, *The Saga of the People of Laxardale* and *Egil's Saga* provide unusually detailed examples of another common motif in sagas of Icelanders: the *Landnám*, the taking or settlement of land in Iceland. After this point, the two sagas diverge: *The Saga of the People of Laxardale* follows the fates of the descendants of Unn the Deep-Minded all the way to the eleventh century; *Egil's Saga* focuses on the life and times of one individual. Much of *Egil's Saga* takes place in Norway and England. Yet another pattern is found in *The Saga of the People of Eyri* (*Eyrbyggja saga*), where the history of an entire region is explored.

"History" does not truly describe the sagas of Icelanders. They might better be described as "crossover fiction"—not simply historical novels, but fictively developed narratives of the intimate lives of men and women, most of whom actually existed. The Icelanders of the thirteenth and fourteenth centuries who wrote, heard, or read these sagas were experiencing stories about their own predecessors and ancestors. What did these sagas mean to them? Modern readers still find the human drama of the saga-world compelling. The drama may be tragic, as in the failed love affair in *The Saga of Gunnlaug Serpent-Tongue*. The scale of *Njal's Saga* is epic. Complex, tormented women such as Gudrun Osvifrsdaughter or Hallgerd Longlegs demand a sophisticated response from the reader.

The thematic range of the sagas of Icelanders is wide, as is evident in the classification provided in box 4.6.

BOX 4.6   *The Sagas of Icelanders*

....

Source: as classified in *The Complete Sagas of Icelanders*, general ed. Viðar Hreinsson, 5 vols. (Reykjavík: Leifur Eiriksson Publishing, 1997).

"These five volumes contain the first complete, coordinated English translation of *The Sagas of Icelanders*, forty in all...." (Preface, *The Complete Sagas of Icelanders*)

Epic

Njal's Saga	Brennu-Njáls saga
The Saga of the People of Laxardale	Laxdæla saga

Champions and Rogues

The Saga of Finnbogi the Mighty	Finnboga saga ramma
The Saga of the People of Floi	Flóamanna saga
The Saga of Gold Thorir	Gull-Þóris saga
The Saga of Gunnar, the Fool of Keldugnup	Gunnars saga Keldugnúpsfífls
The Saga of the People of Kjalarnes	Kjalnesinga saga
The Saga of Ref the Sly	Króka-Refs saga
The Saga of Thord Menace	Þórðar saga hreðu

Wealth and Power

The Saga of the Confederates	Bandamanna saga
The Saga of the People of Eyri	Eyrbyggja saga
The Saga of Havard of Isafjord	Hávarðar saga Ísfirðings
The Saga of Hrafnkel Frey's Godi	Hrafnkels saga Freysgoði
Hen-Thorir's Saga	Hænsna-Þóris saga
Olkofri's Saga	Ölkofra saga

Outlaws and Nature Spirits

Bard's Saga	Bárðar saga Snæfellsáss
Gisli Sursson's Saga	Gísla saga Súrssonar
The Saga of Grettir the Strong	Grettis saga
The Saga of Hord and the People of Holm	Harðar saga ok Hólmverja

Regional Feuds

The Saga of Droplaug's Sons	Droplaugarsona saga
The Saga of the People of Fljotsdal	Fljótsdæla saga
The Saga of the Slayings on the Heath	Heiðarvíga saga

The Saga of the People of Ljosvatn	Ljósvetninga saga
The Saga of the People of Reykjadal and of Killer-Skuta	Reykdœla saga ok Víga-Skútu
The Saga of the People of Svarfardal	Svarfdœla saga
Valla Ljot's Saga	Valla-Ljóts saga
The Saga of the People of Vatnsdal	Vatnsdœla saga
The Saga of the People of Vopnafjord	Vápnfirðinga saga
The Saga of Thorstein the White	Þorsteins saga hvíta
Thorstein Sidu Hallsson's Saga	Þorsteins saga Síðu-Hallssonar

Warriors and Poets

The Saga of Bjorn, Champion of the Hitardal People	Bjarnar saga Hítdœlakappa
Egil's Saga	Egils saga Skalla-Grímssonar
The Saga of the Sworn Brothers	Fóstbrœðra saga
The Saga of Gunnlaug Serpent-Tongue	Gunnlaugs saga ormstungu
The Saga of Hallfred, the Troublesome Poet	Hallfreðar saga vandræðaskáld
Kormak's Saga	Kormáks saga
Killer-Glum's Saga	Víga-Glúms saga
Viglund's Saga	Víglundar saga

Vinland and Greenland

Eirik the Red's Saga	Eiríks saga rauða
The Saga of the Greenlanders	Grœnlendinga saga

The relationship between the later manuscripts of the sagas of Icelanders and the events of the Saga Age is problematic. Controversy on this topic is dominated by two major schools of thought: book prose theory and free prose theory.

Free prose theory regards the sagas as the product of an oral prose tradition, with strong roots in local or regional history. Some claim that the sagas existed in a developed form before they were written down; others see the sagas as having developed from short oral narratives. According to free prose theory, each of the sagas of Icelanders may be regarded as a carefully worked collection of the stories told about an individual or family. Icelanders could read the glorious histories of their own ancestors in the sagas; the theory has often been associated with affirmations of Icelandic exceptionalism and identity from the nineteenth century onwards. Free prose theory treats the sagas as the product of enduring local memory.

Broadly, *book prose theory* sees the sagas of Icelanders as the work of imaginative and learned writers, mainly from the thirteenth and fourteenth centuries. Such writers were brilliant compilers of sagas based on historical works such as *The Book of Settlements* (*Landnámabók*) and kings' sagas. The business of scholarship was to establish manuscript traditions and authoritative versions of texts on the assumption that the production of sagas was always chiefly the product of a literate culture. This theory also lent support to the emerging sense of Icelandic identity and independence as it revealed a medieval Iceland with a complex literary culture that was the equal of any in Europe (see Andersson 1967; Sigurðsson 2004).

Yet another view regards the sagas of Icelanders as having the troubled state of thirteenth-century Iceland as their unstated focus, either as commentary on thirteenth-century events, or as an expression of nostalgia for a better time.

Every saga is unique, but Theodore Andersson (1967 and 2006) has usefully analyzed recurring structural and rhetorical patterns in the sagas of Icelanders. The fundamental structural pattern, according to Andersson, is the following: introduction, conflict, climax, revenge, reconciliation, aftermath. Andersson and others describe the sagas as being stylistically understated, with grammatically straightforward sentences and an almost invisible narrator who has no direct sense of the interiority of the characters in the story.

Useful as such analyses are, each saga must be read on its own terms. For instance, although the above analysis fits the plot of *The Saga of the People of Laxardale*, that saga is unique in its array of extraordinary women. The structure outlined by Andersson proves extremely flexible in its ability to accommodate thematic diversity.

Kings' Sagas / Konungasögur

Kings' sagas record the actions of Scandinavian kings from mythological prehistory until the thirteenth century. Most were written in Iceland or recorded in Icelandic manuscripts. While Latin was the customary language of medieval historiography on the Continent, most Scandinavian royal lives and histories were written in the vernacular. The influence of Ari Thorgilsson the Wise (1067–1148) may be crucial in this matter. His *The Book of Icelanders* (*Íslendingabók*) records the history of Iceland from the settlement to his own time. In it he refers to an earlier, now lost, version of the work, which contained material on royal history. Ari may have established the tradition of vernacular historiography, although it is impossible to tell what formal influence his royal history had on the development of kings' sagas. Certainly, later writers admit a debt to his work.

Another twelfth-century Icelander, Sæmundr Sigfusson the Wise (d. 1133), is also acknowledged as an early writer of royal history. It is likely that he wrote in Latin, but none of his work has survived.

Twelfth-century Norway produced two Latin histories, *Historia de antiquitate regum Norwegiensum* by the monk Theodoricus, and the anonymous *Historia Norvegiae*. Both belong to a European tradition of historiography. In the same period, *An Outline of the Histories of Norwegian Kings (Ágrip af Nóregskonunga sögum)*, written in Norway, continued the vernacular tradition. These texts are all brief lives or synoptic histories.

The Icelandic writer of *Morkinskinna* (Rotten Vellum), ca 1220, produced a monumental history of the Norwegian kings from Saint Olaf (1025) until its abrupt end in the mid-twelfth century. *Morkinskinna* might best be regarded as a sequence or collection of sagas rather than a single saga. The structure is not straightforward, but fascinatingly digressive, and includes many *þættir* or short stories, usually concerned with the successes of Icelanders overseas. Written shortly after *Morkinskinna*, *Fagrskinna* (Fair Vellum) is another text that should be seen as a sequence of sagas. Like its predecessor, *Fagrskinna* contains a large number of skaldic verses, which corroborate the prose narrative since the poems are ostensibly contemporary with the events they describe.

The best known of kings' sagas is *Heimskringla* (lit. *The Circle of the World* but usually referred to by its Icelandic title), ca 1230, generally attributed to Snorri Sturluson (1179–1241). *Heimskringla* begins with *The Saga of the Ynglings* (*Ynglinga saga*), a mythological prehistory of legendary and semi-legendary kings of Sweden and Norway. The remainder of *Heimskringla* comprises the sagas of Norwegian rulers from Halfdan the Black (ca 810–ca 860, king of the Vestfold district of Norway) to Magnus Erlingsson (1156–84, king of Norway). Snorri's work was once regarded as historically reliable, but modern scholars use it with considerable caution.

Snorri used several sources, among them Ari Thorgilsson, *Morkinskinna*, the twelfth-century Latin histories, and the lost *Hryggjarstykki* (Backbone-piece). Snorri's sagas (like other earlier sagas) quote many skaldic praise-poems, contemporary with their subjects, as corroboration of the narrative. The centerpiece of *Heimskringla* is *The Saga of Saint Olaf*, which draws upon an earlier anonymous *The Legendary Life of Saint Olaf* (*Helgisagan*). Oral accounts of kings' lives almost certainly existed, and Snorri may have used some of these. Snorri had himself visited Norway and Sweden.

Heimskringla is vivid and entertaining. The narrative is rich with dialogue and exciting incidents, many of which are quite improbable. The other collections similarly mix historical detail with dramatically appropriate dialogue and incident. Such dialogue and incident may well be part of an oral tradition rather than simply the invention of the saga-writer.

The Saga of the Family of Cnut (*Knýtlinga saga*) deals with the kings of Denmark and was written in the 1250s, probably by an Icelander. There is evidence to suggest that Olaf Thordarson Hvitaskald (the White Skald; d. ca 1259), Snorri Sturluson's nephew, was the author. He also wrote *The Third Grammatical Treatise*, a rhetorical handbook.

Not all kings' sagas, however, were parts of sequences. For instance, *Sverrir's Saga* (*Sverris saga*) is free-standing and was probably written with the guidance of King Sverrir himself (ca 1145/51–1202). The author of at least part of it was Karl Jónsson, an Icelandic monk. At the same time another Icelandic monk, Oddr Snorrason, was engaged in writing a Latin life of Olaf Tryggvason, which survives only in an Icelandic translation. *The Saga of Hakon Hakonarson* (*Hákonar saga Hákonarsonar*) should be seen as coming at the end of the tradition of kings' sagas. Snorri Sturluson's nephew, Sturla Thordarson (1214–84), wrote it at the request of Hakon's successor, Magnus. Though the saga differs in many respects from the earlier, it has a fascinating echoic and intertextual relationship with several of them. Sturla also wrote *The Saga of the Icelanders* (*Íslendinga saga*) in *The Saga of the Sturlungs* (*Sturlunga saga*; see below) as well as compiling a version of *The Book of Settlements* (*Landnámabók*).

Why so many kings' sagas? Why so many by Icelanders, who had left kings behind them? These sagas are not simply chronicles; most of them use narrative to test ideas of kingship, to explore what constitutes a good or bad king. Norwegian kings (and one or two Danes) had a rather proprietorial attitude toward Iceland: there is some suggestion that Snorri, for example, is anti-monarchical. Despite his devious politics, Snorri is a balanced and clear-sighted observer of royal behavior (Jacobsson 2005). Saxo Grammaticus, ca 1200, argued that, since Icelanders lived impoverished lives in a land without natural resources, their culture took a literary form; for that, one needs only cattle (the raw material of vellum) and ink.

A few other sagas are loosely classified with kings' sagas. *The Saga of the Jomsvikings* (*Jómsvíkinga saga*) narrates the history of the semi-legendary Viking brotherhood of Jomsborg, from its foundation in the tenth century until its defeat at the hands of Jarl Hakon at the Battle of Hjörungavag in 986. *The Saga of the Orkney Islanders* (*Orkneyinga saga*), written by an Icelander ca 1200, is a stirring account of the earls of Orkney and includes memorable figures such as Thorfinn the Mighty and Svein Asleifarson. This saga is also memorable for its use of the poetry of Arnor Jarlaskald (Skald of Earls). *The Saga of the Faeroe Islanders* (*Færeyinga saga*), ca 1200, recounts the settlement and history of the Faeroes. *The Saga of the Gotlanders* (*Guta saga*), from the thirteenth century, contains the early history of Gotland reaching back to the migration period. Later passages define Gotland's independent relationship with Sweden.

Contemporary Sagas / Samtíðarsögur, Samtímasögur

As their name implies, these sagas are regarded as having been written close in time to the events they narrate, mainly in late twelfth- and thirteenth-century Iceland. This age was known as the Age of the Sturlungs (*Sturlungaöld*). The Sturlung family came to prominence with the rise of Hvamm-Sturla in the late twelfth century. The period of Sturlung power saw the rapid slide of Iceland into a ferocious civil war, which ended only with the submission of Iceland to Norway in 1262. *The Saga of the Sturlungs* (*Sturlunga saga*) is a compendium of sagas covering the events of the period. Their contemporary composition suggests that they may be more reliable history than the sagas of Icelanders.

Part of *Sturlunga saga* is *The Saga of the Icelanders* (*Íslendinga saga*) written by Sturla Thordarson, Snorri's nephew. Sturla provides a powerful account of events that he himself experienced. Nonetheless, his history contains much foreshadowing of disasters, warning dreams, and other motifs appropriate to what would now be regarded as fiction. Sturla's *The Saga of the Icelanders* should not be confused with the sagas of Icelanders discussed above.

Bishops' Sagas

After Christianization, saints' lives began to be translated into Icelandic. The lives of Thomas Becket and Mary were among the *heilagra manna sögur* (tales of saintly people) that appeared in Icelandic. When Iceland produced its own saints, their *vitae* (lives) were translated into Icelandic. These saints were also bishops, so the production of saints' lives should not be distinguished too sharply from the writing of the lives of early Icelandic bishops. Bishops' sagas are more than collections of wonders: they provide information on the development of Icelandic Christianity and the increasing importance of bishops.

Legendary Sagas / Fornaldarsögur

These sagas are set in the old world before the Saga Age (i.e., before ca 870) and are inhabited by trolls, giants, dwarves, and ferocious kings: Magic abounds. As well as such obviously mythological elements, the sagas sometimes contain echoes of historical events. Ragnar Hairy-Breeches (*Loðbrók*) and his sons were historical characters, though little of their actual doings remains in their saga. *Hervarar saga* is, however, of particular relevance to early Swedish history. The legendary sagas do sometimes fill gaps in other forms of Norse literature. One legendary saga, *The Saga of the Volsungs*, for example, contains material not found in *The Poetic Edda*.

Short Story / þáttr

Literally, the term *þáttr* (pl. *þættir*) means a single strand of a rope and is extended to mean a section of a text, such as a law code. The term is also applied to short identifiable narratives included in more extensive sagas. Typically in a *þáttr*, an Icelander arrives at a foreign court (frequently, the Norwegian court) and distinguishes himself by his talents or character. *The Story of Audun from the Westfjords* (*Auðunar þáttr vestfirzka*), for example, tells how a simple Icelander goes to Greenland, where he buys a polar bear with the intention of giving it to the king of Denmark, which he succeeds in doing. Naturally, the king rewards him abundantly. A version of this short story is embedded in the *Saga of King Magnus and King Harald* (*Saga Magnúsar konungs ok Haralds konungs*) in a large anthology called *The Book of Flatey* (*Flateyjarbók*).

There has been some speculation that sagas were originally woven from such disparate strands, which might have been easily transmitted orally. The structure of the surviving *þættir* is generally so distinctive, however, that it is difficult to imagine how the diversity of existing sagas could have arisen in this way (Andersson 1967). Another possibility is that *þættir* were intended to exemplify or illustrate the main narrative from which they digress (Clover 1982).

Icelandic Historical Texts

Ari the Wise (inn Fróði) Thorgilsson, the earliest-known Icelandic historian, wrote *The Book of Icelanders* (*Íslendingabók*; *Libellus Islandorum*) between 1122 and 1133. Remarkably, he chose to write his history of Iceland in the vernacular, even though Latin was the usual vehicle for history in the Middle Ages and Ari's work reveals him to be an educated man who knew Latin. Ari's choice must be seen as a major influence on the subsequent development of Icelandic historiography, which followed his lead in the use of the vernacular.

His introduction indicates that Ari had written an earlier, now lost history of Iceland and that it contained material concerning the kings of Norway. The surviving version, however, does not give any royal history. It is impossible to judge the effect of this lost text on the later development of kings' sagas. He may also have written an early version of *The Book of Settlements* (*Landnámabók*). Ari, as a careful historian, opens by explaining why he wrote his book and continues by discussing his sources and his reasons for regarding them as trustworthy. He is careful in establishing a rational chronology for his history.

The Book of Icelanders begins with the settlement of Iceland (ca 870) and ends in Ari's own time (ca 1120). It may be that Ari should be credited with the Icelandic foundation story that regards the settlement of Iceland as a Norwegian undertaking; he has nothing to say of migrants from Scotland or Ireland. Like Ari's work, many sagas begin by discussing Harald Finehair, though Ari does not regard Harald as having driven men into flight. To some extent, Ari's history has a narrow focus on the history of his own family rather than on the settlement as a whole. In addition, his account of the conversion is strangely secular, appearing more concerned with the conversion as a legal procedure than as a change of faith (Grønlie 2006). Indeed, Ari's legal and political focus manifests itself in the considerable space he allocates to the establishment of law, the foundation of the Althing, and the division of Iceland into quarters.

The Book of Icelanders is terse to a fault. Ari, in all probability, had no vernacular models to follow, so he sometimes wrestles with the difficulties of producing formal prose in a language without a written prose tradition. Nonetheless, his influence is acknowledged by the major Icelandic writers who followed him (Grønlie 2006).

The author of The History of the Conversion (Kristni saga) had read The Book of Icelanders but approaches the conversion from a different point of view. The History of the Conversion, which probably dates from the middle of the thirteenth century, is much more an ecclesiastical or missionary history than Ari's, with a more spiritual and moral attitude about the change of faith. There has been considerable speculation about the identity of the author, with Sturla Thordarson as a favored candidate (Grønlie 2006).

A third source that should be mentioned here is The Book of Settlements (Landnámabók), an early version of which may have been written by Ari Thorgilsson. The Book of Settlements survives in several versions, the most important of which are Sturlubók, written by Sturla Thordarson in the latter part of the thirteenth century, and Hauksbók, written by Haukr Erlendsson and included in his huge anthology with the same title, which dates from the early fourteenth century. Sturla Thordarson was the nephew of Snorri Sturluson, the saga-writer and mythographer. Sturla was also responsible for The Saga of the Icelanders (Íslendinga saga), one of the most compelling parts of The Saga of the Sturlungs, which narrates Iceland's devastating civil war. Perhaps his version of The Book of Settlements was designed to form part of an ambitious complete history of Iceland.

The Book of Settlements records the arrival and settlement of the founders of the more prominent Icelandic families from ca 874 until ca 930, when the settlement period was regarded as complete, yet many family histories are extended to the eleventh and twelfth centuries. Sturla based his work on the lost Styrmisbók by Styrmir Kárason (d. 1245).

The Book of Settlements repeats the foundation story that Iceland was settled by honorable Norwegians in flight from Harald Finehair. There can be no doubt of its immense historical value, yet the surviving versions appear at the time when the writing of Icelandic sagas was approaching its zenith. *The Book of Settlements* contains many brief narratives that sound very much like the germs, or perhaps the fruit, of the sagas of Icelanders. The direction of the influence is difficult to trace, if, indeed, there is only one direction. It is as difficult to use *The Book of Settlements* to substantiate the sagas as it is to do the reverse. For example, the account of Skallagrim's Landtake in *Sturlubók* may well have been influenced by the version found in *Egil's Saga* (ch. 28).

Nonetheless, *The Book of Settlements* documents the arrival in Iceland of around 400 prominent families and provides an unusual insight into the social effects of their adaptation to the new environment. *The Book of Settlements* suggests that original social distinctions were to some degree leveled in the process of settlement, a suggestion substantiated by the social conditions described in many of the sagas of Icelanders.

BOX 4.7 **Íslendingabók (The Book of Icelanders)** *on the Settlement of Iceland*

Source: Trans. A.A. Somerville, from *Íslendingabók*, ed. Jakob Benediktsson, Íslenzk Fornrit I (Reykjavík, 1986), pp. 4–7.

1. Iceland was first settled from Norway in the days of King Harald Finehair, the son of Halfdan the Black. According to the reckoning of the wisest man I know—my foster-father Teit, son of Bishop Isleif—and of my uncle, Thorkel Gellisson, who remembered a long way back, and of Thurid, daughter of Snorri the Priest, who was both wise and well-informed, the settlement of Iceland took place at the time when Ivarr, the son of Ragnar Hairy-Breeches, had Saint Edmund, king of the English, killed. And according to Saint Edmund's saga, that happened 870 years after the birth of Christ.

The story goes—and it is a true one—that a Norwegian, called Ingolf, traveled from Norway to Iceland for the first time when Harald Finehair was 16 years old and, again, a few years later. He settled to the south, in Reykjavik. The place where he landed first is called Ingolf's Head, to the east of Minthak's Shoal, and the place where he later settled is Ingolfsfell, which lies to the east of the Olfoss river.

In those days, there were trees growing in Iceland between the mountains and the shore. There were also Christian men here, whom the Norsemen called *papar*, but they left afterwards because they did not want to live alongside heathens. They left behind some Irish books, bells, and croziers, from which it may be deduced that they were Irishmen.

After that, a great number of people began to migrate here from Norway until King Harald banned the practice, fearing that his land would be depopulated otherwise. Then it was agreed that anyone coming here from Norway would have to pay the king five pieces of gold, unless he was granted an exemption. King Harald is said to have been king for 70 years and to have reached the age of 80.

This is the origin of the tax called Landaurar [Land money]. The tax was sometimes higher and sometimes lower until Olaf the Stout [Saint Olaf, 995–1030] made it definite that anyone traveling between Norway and Iceland had to pay the king half a mark, except for women and the men he exempted. Thorkell Gellisson was our source for this.

THE ART OF POETRY

Old Norse eddic (heroic and mythological) poetry offers indispensable insights into the ethical, religious, and social values of the culture that produced it. Skaldic poetry celebrates the deeds of historical Norse rulers and warriors, and involves the individual subject in a richly rhetorical web of cultural allusion. Both kinds of poetry testify to an astonishingly sophisticated textual culture.

Germanic poetry began as an oral poetry, and its Viking Age descendants retain many formal features that recall their oral origins. Naturally, our knowledge of Viking Age poetry is drawn from written versions whose closeness to oral poetry can only be guessed at, and poems with features suggestive of an earlier orality may well have begun their lives on the manuscript page. The Old Norse use of alliteration in combination with patterns of stress-accent is distinctly Germanic and suggests roots in oral poetry. The alliteration is almost certainly mnemonic in function and, in combination with stress, highlights the most important elements of the line, in a manner useful to hearer and poet alike.

Kinds of Old Norse Poetry

As introduced above, Old Norse poetry falls into two major classes, distinguished mainly by the meters used in each type. While most scholars make this distinction, it is important to remember that subject matter sometimes overlaps.

Eddic Poetry/Eddukvæði

This is the early heroic and mythological poetry that comprises *The Poetic Edda*, a group of poems contained chiefly in one late thirteenth-century Icelandic manuscript known as the Codex Regius (King's Book). While the Codex Regius was produced in Iceland during the latter part of the thirteenth century, the poetry is older and may have originated elsewhere in Scandinavia. One heroic poem in the manuscript, *Atlamál* (The Poem of Atli), is said to be of Greenlandic origin. The Danish historian Saxo Grammaticus (ca 1200) acknowledged his debt to Icelandic poetry, but he also used material drawn from unknown sources, which may or may not have been Icelandic. Snorri Sturluson used many of the poems that appear in *The Poetic Edda* as the basis of his own prose version of Norse mythology in his *Prose Edda* (ca 1240). His sources are unknown, but he may have had access to an anthology very like the Codex Regius. Another possibility is that he knew some of the poems in oral form. Eddic poetry employs *fornyrðislag*, or *old meter*, and its variants, which are formally very close to Anglo-Saxon meter, indicate their shared background in Germanic poetry. Eddic poetry is usually anonymous.

BOX 4.8   *Fornyrðislag: The Meter of Eddic Poetry*

The line (*vísuorð*) in *fornyrðislag* has four syllables usually, two of which are stressed. One or two stressed syllables of every odd line alliterate with the first stressed syllable of the following even line. For example, lines 1 and 2 of *Atlakviða* (*The Story of Attila* from *The Poetic Edda*) are in *fornyrðislag*. In the following example, the symbol / indicates a stressed syllable and x an unstressed; alliterating syllables are italicized and bolded. Here, the alliterating syllables open with vowels, all of which may alliterate with one another:

/ x / x
A*tli sendi*   Atli sent

/ x   / x
á*r til Gunnars.*   a messenger to Gunnar.

A common variant of *fornyrðislag* is *málaháttr* (speech measure), which differs in having five or six syllables in a line. For example, lines 7 and 8 of *Atlakviða*:

  /   /
D*rucco þar **d**róttmegir*   The warriors drank there,

/   /
enn **d**yliendr þǫgðo   concealed their thoughts in silence

Both *fornyrðislag* and *málaháttr* are arranged in stanzas, usually of eight lines.

Ljóðaháttr (song measure) is another common variant of *fornyrðislag*, in which two lines of *fornyrðislag* are followed by a three-stressed line, twice in each stanza. This popular eddic meter occurs in *Hávamál*, from which the following stanza is taken (as is often the case, several of the *fornyrðislag* lines are shortened, having as few as two syllables):

/ /
Deyr fé,   Cattle die,

/ x /
deyja frændr;   Kin die;

/ / x / x
deyr siálfr it sama: self dies too;

/ x /
ek veit einn   but I do know

x / x /
at aldri deyr,   what never dies,

/ x / x /
dómr um dauðan hvern   the glory of the deeds of the dead.

The terms *málaháttr* and *ljóðaháttr* imply that the poetry in these measures is close to speech and chant or song. Many eddic poems present direct speech and dialogue, while others resemble incantations, or even work songs.

The Poetic Edda

Mythological Poetry from the Codex Regius
(*Konungsbók*, Royal Book)

Sayings of Grimnir	*Grímnismál*
The Journey of Skirnir	*Skírnismál*
The Lay of Harbard	*Hárbarðsljóð*
Hymir's Poem	*Hymiskviða*
The Flyting of Loki	*Lokasenna*
Thrym's Poem	*Þrymskviða*
Völund's Poem	*Völundarkviða*
Sayings of All-wise	*Alvíssmál*

The poems in this part of the manuscript powerfully suggest the circumstances of oral delivery, since direct speech and dialogue are the typical modes employed. The first four poems focus on Odin's quest for knowledge, particularly about Ragnarök, the Doom of the Gods. In the first, the Seeress (*völva*) answers implied questions from Odin. Readers are not *told* about the Seeress's prophecy in *Völuspá*; they hear her speak. Her prophecy is, in fact, a history of the world from creation to Ragnarök. Similarly, Odin gives us advice in his own voice and tells us of how he suffered as the hanged god to gain wisdom in *Hávamál*. *Vafþrúðnismál* is almost entirely a dialogue between Odin and a giant, Vafthrudnir, and suggests a performance rather than a text to be read. Again, the subject matter is mythological.

Another group presents Thor. In *Hárbarðsljóð*, he exchanges verbal abuse in a flyting (a formal exchange of insults) with the disguised Odin. *Hymiskviða* contains a version of the adventure in which Thor fishes for the World Serpent. *Þrymskviða* sends Thor in female disguise on a quest to regain his stolen hammer. The final Thor poem is *Alvíssmál*, a battle of wits between Thor and a dwarf.

The anthology has a structure, but it is not rigidly maintained. Between the Odin and Thor groups *Skírnismál* interrupts with the unrelated tale of how Skirnir comes to woo Gerd (a giantess) on behalf of Freyr. *Lokasenna* is placed immediately before *Þrymskviða* in the Thor group; it is an exchange of abuse between Loki and the other gods. Loki has been denied an invitation to a party held by the gods, but he comes along anyway and takes the opportunity to heap often scurrilous abuse on the other gods, who reply in kind. Interestingly, the manuscript provides marginal indications of each speaker's part, a feature highly suggestive of drama.

Between *Þrymskviða* and *Alvíssmál* is *Völundarkviða*, the story of Völund (Weland) the Smith. The poem tells of Völund's marriage with a swan-maiden and his loneliness after she leaves him. He is captured by King Nithod, who cuts Völund's hamstrings to prevent his escape, and forces him to produce marvelous smith's work for him. Völund's revenge (the murder of Nithod's sons and the rape of his daughter) brings the tale to an end. *Völundarkviða* is a splendid poem, but why does it occupy this position in the manuscript? *Skírnismál* and

Lokasenna raise the same question. The compiler of the manuscript was orderly; did he make connections that are not apparent to us?

Heroic Poetry from the Codex Regius

The Helgi Poems

The First Lay of Helgi Hundingsbani	
(Slayer of Hunding)	*Helgakviða Hundingsbana I*
The Lay of Helgi Hjörvardsson	*Helgakviða Hjörvarðssonar*
The Second Lay of Helgi Hundingsbani	*Helgakviða Hundingsbana II*

The Lay of Helgi Hundingsbani I and *II* are perhaps versions of the same poem, recounting the exploits of the hero Helgi, son of Sigmund the Völsung, and his love affair with a valkyrie. Valkyries were "choosers of the slain" who ferried chosen dead heroes to Valhalla, Odin's great hall. Some were goddesses, while others (as in these poems) were mortals who opted for the valkyrie life. *Helgi* means "sacred one," suggesting a mythic relationship with the choosers of the slain. The tale of Helgi Hjörvardsson resembles the others in subject matter, but confusingly the hero has a different paternity.

The Lay of Helgi Hundingsbani I ends with Helgi's marriage to his valkyrie. In *The Lay of Helgi Hundingsbani II*, however, the slain Helgi and his valkyrie have a last meeting in his burial mound. The text ends by suggesting that they will be reincarnated. *The Lay of Helgi Hjörvardsson* (son of Hjorvard) recounts the death of Helgi. Helgi bequeaths his valkyrie to his half-brother Hedin, who has already taken an unfortunate vow to marry her. Each poem has a splendid *flyting* or formal exchange of insults between two characters, as in *Lokasenna*. The flytings sometimes hint at abnormal behavior and sexual deviancy.

Völsungs and Niflungs

On the Death of Sinfjötli [prose passage]	*Frá dauða Sinfjötla*
Gripir's Prophecy	*Grípisspá*
The Lay of Regin	*Reginsmál*
The Lay of Fafnir	*Fáfnismál*
The Lay of Sigrdrifa	*Sigrdrífumál*
Fragment of a Poem about Sigurd	*Brot af Sigurðarkviðu*
The First Lay of Gudrun	*Guðrúnarkviða I*
The Short Lay of Sigurd	*Sigurðarkviða hin skamma*
Brynhild's Hell-Ride	*Helreið Brynhildar*
The Slaughter of the Niflungs	
[prose passage]	*Dráp Niflunga*
The Second Lay of Gudrun	*Guðrúnarkviða II*

The Third Lay of Gudrun	*Guðrúnarkviða III*
Oddrun's Lament	*Oddrúnargrátr*
The Lay of Atli [Attila]	*Atlakviða*
The Greenlandic Poem of Atli	*Atlamál*
The Incitement of Gudrun	*Guðrúnarhvöt*
The Lay of Hamdir	*Hamðismál*

This group presents the most familiar Germanic heroic legends, the tales of the Völsungs and the story of the Niflungs (Nibelungs). *On the Death of Sinfjötli* is a prose summary of early Völsung history. The first five poems chronicle the Völsungs and focus on Sigurd the Völsung, the slayer of the dragon, Fafnir. *Gripir's Prophecy* foresees the content of the next four poems, which narrate the origin of the Rhine Gold and the slaying of the dragon, Fafnir, by Sigurd. In *The Lay of Sigrdrifa*, Sigurd receives instruction on the use of the runes by the valkyrie, Sigrdrifa.

In *Fragment of a Poem about Sigurd*, the brothers of his wife, Gudrun the Niflung, murder Sigurd, at the instigation of the valkyrie Brynhild, enraged that he married Gudrun rather than herself. *The First Lay of Gudrun* is a powerful treatment of Gudrun's inability to weep for her husband. Several women tell dreadful tales of their own experiences in war in an effort to help her release her grief in tears. *The Short Lay of Sigurd* moves to the other woman in the affray, Brynhild the valkyrie. She had been deceived into marrying Gunnar, brother of Gudrun, in the place of Sigurd who had promised to marry her. In a powerful scene, she stabs herself and joins Sigurd in death on her funeral pyre. Before dying, she looks into the gloomy future of the Niflungs. Immediately afterwards comes *Brynhild's Hell-Ride*, which recounts a conversation between Brynhild and a giantess encountered on the road to Hel.

Next follow poems concerning Gudrun's dealings with Atli (Attila the Hun) and Jörmunrekkr (Ermanaric the Goth), particularly their bloodier episodes. The poems are introduced by a prose summary, *The Slaughter of the Niflungs*. *The Second Lay of Gudrun* is in dialogue form. Gudrun recounts her life from the murder of Sigurd until her present marriage to Atli. She makes gloomy prophecies of the fall of the Niflungs through the murder of her brothers, Gunnar and Högni, by Atli. *The Third Lay of Gudrun* finds Gudrun falsely accused of adultery. The accusations rebound on the false witness who is punished by being drowned in a bog.

Oddrun's Lament is the complaint of Atli's sister, Oddrun, who had hoped to marry Sigurd and feels that she was cheated by everyone around her.

The Lay of Atli and *The Greenlandic Poem of Atli* give similar accounts of Atli's murder of Gudrun's brothers, Gunnar and Högni. *The Lay of Atli* is an austere narration of horrors, relying on loosely linked episodes to describe the major events. *The Greenlandic Poem of Atli* is considerably more bloodstained and sensational. Though forewarned by their sister, Gunnar and Högni accept an invitation to visit Atli, who intends to force the treasure of the Niflungs from them. They die horribly without revealing the location of the treasure. In the final episode of both poems, Gudrun serves up her sons by Atli as "ale-dainties" before dinner. Then she informs the drunken Atli of her revenge for his murder of her brothers. She kills him and burns down the palace.

In *The Incitement of Gudrun,* Gudrun shames the sons of her third marriage into taking revenge on Ermanaric who has had Svanhild, Gudrun's daughter by Sigurd, trampled to death by horses. In *The Lay of Hamdir,* two of her sons, Hamdir and Sörli, murder Ermanaric by chopping off his hands and feet. Unfortunately, they had murdered the third brother, Erp, en route; had he been with them, he would have cut off Ermanaric's head, which would have prevented him from ordering his men to stone them to death, the only means of killing them. Gudrun and her sons recognize that her revenge has hurt her as much as the targets of the act of vengeance.

The poems concerning Atli and Jörmunrekkr are loosely related to late fourth- and fifth-century Germanic history, but the chronology is confused and the value of the texts does not rest in their witness to historical events. Though Gunnar's tribe, the Burgundians, fought with the Huns, there is nothing to suggest that Attila himself was involved. Though Ermanaric dies after Attila in the poems, the reverse is the case in fact.

Eddic Poetry Not in the Codex Regius

Mythological Poetry

Baldur's Dreams (*Baldrs draumar*): Odin asks a seeress to explain Baldur's bad
  dreams. She foresees the deaths of both Baldur and Odin.
The Lay of Rig (*Rígsþula*): The god Heimdall, adopting the name of Rig,
  visits and goes to bed with a series of couples, thus creating the social
  classes. The classes are vividly described by appearance, occupation,
  and diet.
The Song of Hyndla (*Hyndluljóð*): The goddess Freyja and the giantess
  Hyndla discuss the ancestry of Freyja's favorite.
The Short Prophecy of the Seeress (*Völuspá in skamma*): This poem covers some
  of the material of the later part of *Völuspá*.
The Lay of Svipdag (*Svipdagsmál*) is formed from two shorter poems:
  Gróa's Spell (*Grógaldr*); *The Lay of Fjölsvid* (*Fjölsvinnsmál*): Svipdag
    searches for the girl Menglöd, who is necessary for his happiness.
The Song of Grotti (*Gróttasöngr*): Two female slaves use a magical mill,
  Grotti, to produce whatever is desired by their owner, a Danish king.

At last they rebel against his insatiable greed and grind out an army to overthrow him.

Odins's Raven Chant (Hrafnagaldur Óðins): This poem is widely regarded as a later imitation of eddic poetry. Gloomy echoes of *The Prophecy of the Seeress* suggest that the end of the world is close. To discover the meaning of the many ominous signs, Odin sends messengers to visit Hel.

Heroic Poetry

The Waking of Angantyr and *The Lay of Hlöd (Hlöðskviða)*, also known as *The Battle of the Goths and the Huns*: both of these poems are found in *Hervarar saga*. In the first, Hervor awakes her dead father Angantyr and asks him for his magic sword. In the second, Hervor's sons, Hlod and Angantyr, fight over the kingdom of the Goths. The Huns come to the aid of Hlod.

Skaldic Poetry (Poetry of the *Drótt*, or Court)

The poetry of the skalds first appeared during the ninth and tenth centuries and continued to be produced until the fourteenth century. Skaldic poetry usually concerns events roughly contemporary with the poet, who is usually named (unlike the poets of *The Poetic Edda*).

Skaldic poetry was first composed in Norway in the ninth century, but it reached its maturity in Iceland from the early tenth century onwards. Skaldic poets were chiefly court poets and, from the late tenth century, most were Icelanders. Much of their poetry was praise poetry and may be found incorporated in kings' sagas, such as those written by Snorri Sturluson in *Heimskringla*, as well as in *Morkinskinna*, *Fagrskinna*, *Ágrip*, and so on. Snorri and other writers of kings' sagas used skaldic poetry as corroboration of their historical narratives. The prose could be regarded as an amplification of the verse around which it is arranged.

BOX 4.9   *Dróttkvætt: Court Measure*

This favorite measure of the skalds employs alliteration, stress patterns, and internal rhyme and half rhyme.

A *dróttkvætt* stanza contains eight lines, each having six syllables and three stresses. Generally, the stanza falls into two parts of four lines (*helmingr*).

Alliteration: One or two stressed syllables of each odd line will alliterate with the first stressed syllable of the immediately following even line.

Internal rhyme and assonance: In the odd lines, we find half-rhyme, or assonance; that is, two syllables end with the same consonant preceded by a different vowel. In the even lines, there is full-rhyme; that is, two syllables rhyme in both vowel and consonant.

In this example, alliteration is **bold**, half-rhyme is *italic*, and full-rhyme is ***bold italic***. If this poem is of the date and origin claimed for it, it is probably the first European poem composed in North America.

Hafa kva*ð*u **m**ik **m**e*ið*ar	I'd get, they guaranteed it,
malm**þ***ing*s, es komk h*ing*at,	men of the iron-clash, if I
	came here
(**m***ér* samir **l**and f*yr* **l***ý*ðum	—I should curse this coast—
las*t*a) drykk inn b**a***zt*a:	the best of booze;
Bílds h*att*ar verðr b*y*ttu	Tyr's man [the poet] bears a
	bucket,
be*ið*i-**T***ýr* at st*ý*ra;	not the hooded god's helmet;
h**e**l*d*r's svát **k**r*ý*pk at **k**el**d**u—	I creep to the creek,
komat *ví*n á grön m*í*na.	find only water in Wineland.

—Þórhallr Veiðimaðr (Thorhall the Huntsmann), ca 1006
(Tr. A.A. Somerville, from *Eirik the Red's Saga*)

The language of *dróttkvætt* contains rich circumlocutions known as *kennings*, as well as a wide array of near synonyms or *heiti*.

Kenning. A kenning is a circumlocution, a roundabout way of describing or naming something. For example, instead of using the word "battle" or a synonym, the skaldic poet might say "sword storm." "Storm" is the *base word*, and "sword" the *determiner*. These features of skaldic poetry are illustrated in the words of Snorri Sturluson in *The Prose Edda*. The second and third parts (*Skáldskaparmál*/On Poetic Diction and *Háttatal*/List of Meters) are invaluable for their treatment of poetic diction and meter.

On kennings:

Some kennings for gold are: fire of the hand [or arm], fire of the joint, or fire of the arm, because it is red; silver is snow, ice, or frost because it is white. Similarly, gold and silver should be described in terms of the purse, or crucible, or smelter. Both silver and gold may be stones of the arm.... (from *Skáldskaparmál*, chapter 46)

Kennings are divided into three classes. First are [basic] kennings; second are double kennings; third are enlarged kennings. To call battle 'the crashing of spears' is a kenning; to call a sword 'the fire of the crashing of spears' is a double kenning. If it is any longer, it is an enlarged kenning. (from *Háttatal*, chapter 2)

On heiti: *Skáldskaparmál* contains several lists (*þulur*) of names that may be substituted for other terms: for example, *serpent*, from chapter 10.

These are heiti for serpents: dreki, Fáfnir, Jörmungandr, naðr, Níðhöggr, linnr, naðra, Góinn, Móinn, Grafvitnir, Grábakr, Ófnir, Sváfnir, grímr.

Some kennings and heiti in Thorhall the Huntsman's poem on Vínland (see above):
meiðar malmþings = trees of the meeting of iron = warriors
meiðar = trees; often used in poetry to equal *man*
malmþings = of the meeting of iron = of battle
In *bílds hattar*:
bílds = lit., of a spear, often used to signify Odin
hattar = of a hood: thus, of Odin's hood = helmet

Although the diction of skaldic poetry relies heavily on pagan myth, the composition of *dróttkvætt* survived the coming of Christianity. Einarr Skula-son's twelfth-century *Geisli* is a sophisticated combination of skaldic conven-tion with Christian doctrine.

The best-known form of skaldic poem is the *drápa*, from *drepa*, "to strike"; this derivation suggests the striking of a stringed instrument. The *drápa* is a poem of some length with an introduction followed by sections with refrains (*stef*) at regular intervals, and a formal ending. The meter is generally *dróttkvætt* or one of its variants. Much less formally constructed is the *flokkr* or *flock* of *dróttkvætt* stanzas. Gunnlaugr Serpent's-Tongue, an eleventh-century Icelandic skald, considered the *drápa* suitable for kings, while earls must be satisfied with a *flokkr*. Snorri recounts that Cnut the Great was outraged when he received a *flokkr* rather than the expected *drápa*. Much skaldic poetry is preserved in sagas of various kinds as isolated *dróttkvætt* stanzas (*lausavísa*, pl. *lausavísur*).

In general, skaldic poetry is described as praise-poetry (eulogy, panegyric) composed by professional skalds, or court poets. However, this description gives little sense of the thematic range of skaldic poetry. For example, the ninth-century Norwegian Bragi Boddason the Old, the earliest known skald, wrote *Ragnarsdrápa* in thanks for the gift of a shield from King Ragnar Hairy-Breeches. Bragi's poem describes the magnificently executed mythological scenes depicted on the shield. The name *Bragi* is also given to a Norse god of poetry, though Odin is generally regarded as playing that role. The poet's name is also related to the Norse term *bragr*, meaning poetry, what Bragi, god or man, produced.

Poetry of this sort was not offered only to kings. In his *Prose Edda*, Snorri preserves several stanzas from *Húsdrápa* (*Poem in Praise of a House*) by Úlfr Uggason. There is every reason to believe that this is the poem referred to in *The Saga of the People of Laxardale* as having been composed by Úlfr to honor Olaf the Peacock and his new house. On the walls of Olaf's house were carved wooden panels depicting mythological scenes, which form the subject-matter of Ulfr's poem.

Not all skaldic poetry belongs to courts and great houses. Many poems arise directly from the situation of its composer, as is the case with the love-poetry of *Kormak's Saga* or *The Saga of Gunnlaug Serpent's Tongue*. In addition, Egil Skallagrimsson composed his finely made lament *Sonatorrek* (*The Terrible Loss of My Sons*) for the members of his own family. And the rest of *Egil's Saga* is rich with *lausavísur* closely linked to his own actions.

In fact, *Egil's Saga* raises an enduring scholarly problem. Bjarni Einarson (2003) has suggested (and many agree) that Egil is not likely to have composed many (or any) of the poems in his saga. Bjarni attributes the entire saga along with its poetry to Snorri Sturluson, who lived 300 years after Egil. Indeed, skaldic poetry presents enormous problems of dating and origin. *Dróttkvætt* stanzas are tightly constructed and thus, paradoxically, memorable. For, if oral transmission disturbs the structure, the disturbance will be noted. This, of course, is not susceptible to absolute proof, and serious doubts remain. Without doubt there were skaldic poets who composed oral poetry, but is it the poetry attributed to them in the sagas? There is no easy answer, and each case must be argued on its own merits.

There is no complete modern edition of skaldic poetry with English translation and apparatus, though that state of affairs is now being remedied. The Skaldic Poetry Project, housed at the University of Sydney, is in the process of producing just such an edition of the entire skaldic corpus. Two volumes have already appeared: Volume II, Poetry from the Kings' Sagas 2: From c. 1035 to c. 1300 (2009); and Volume VII: Poetry on Christian Subjects (2007). Access to a considerable amount of skaldic poetry is available at the project's website: http://abdn.ac.uk/skaldic/db.php?if=default&table=home&view.

The TEXTS page on the site provides a clickable list of Norse prose texts containing skaldic poetry. The reader has immediate access to the names and works of major skaldic poets in praise of each Norwegian king or earl of

Orkney. The occasional skaldic poems in the various sagas are also listed and accessible. It is impossible to overrate the value of this database, or the fact that so much of it is readily available. Students of the Viking Age have become very rich.

To give two examples: opening the *Heimskringla* section leads the reader to a menu of different ways of accessing the skaldic content. A click on *Haralds saga hárfagra* [*sic*] (*Harald Finehair's Saga*) opens links to the poets and their poems as recorded by Snorri in the saga. This is simply the beginning: keep clicking…there are astonishing finds. The link to *Egils saga Skalla-Grímssonar* leads to the poems of Egil, his father, and his grandfather. This page is edited by Margaret Clunies Ross, a moving force in the entire undertaking. The EDITORS page for the entire site is a list of many of the finest scholars in Norse studies.

Excellent translations of skaldic poetry in the sagas of Icelanders are available in the new Leifur Eiríksson edition. Access to annotated translations is provided by the published texts of the Skaldic Poetry Project. A few translations of kings' sagas also include translations of reasonable quality.

The Delivery of Viking Age Poetry

In *Egil's Saga*, Egil Skallagrimsson is seen reciting his *drápa*, *Head-ransom*, before the court of King Eirik Bloodax, having spent an anxious night working out what to say. King Magnus of Norway and his uncle Harald Hardradi listen to a court poet praising each of them in turn. Frequently, the poet is shown extemporizing the most complex verse, as did Gisli Sursson to his downfall. From an early age, Egil seems to have no trouble in tossing off minor masterpieces without a moment's notice. Though the dating of Norse poetry is often problematic, when Old Norse skaldic poetry is contextualized in the documents in which it appears, it is seen as emphatically oral and public, and, often, as extemporized. Skalds represent themselves as technically proficient rather than inspired. Elsewhere in Germanic poetry, in *Beowulf* for instance, part of the entertainment at a civilized court is the performance of poetry. In *Beowulf*, a poet accompanies himself on a harp. Interestingly, *drápa* is a term that may once have suggested the action of striking, a harp for instance.

The modern period has seen attempts to reconstruct the performance of Old Norse poetry. Icelander Sveinbjörn Beinteinsson (1924–93) recorded performances of eddic poetry and Icelandic *rímur* (ballads). Sveinbjörn also founded *Ásatrúarfélagið* (The Fellowship of the Faith of the Æsir), recognized as a religion in 1973. The Norwegian Black Metal group Burzum has also recorded eddic poetry, while the European ensemble *Sequentia* has recorded scholarly and highly entertaining performances of several eddic poems.

In sum, the paucity of surviving documentary materials produced by Scandinavians in the Viking Age means that scholars are forced to rely either on accounts written by outsiders who were relatively unfamiliar with the Northmen, or on materials that were produced by Scandinavians themselves long after the Viking Age had passed. In both cases, materials must be approached with circumspection, and rigorous standards of source criticism must be employed. Not surprisingly, scholars often disagree on the admissibility of particular sources, but this disagreement provides some of the most stimulating debates on the Vikings.

CHAPTER FIVE

A CASE STUDY EXERCISE: THE WANDERING MONKS OF SAINT PHILIBERT

One of the great pleasures and challenges of the study of the past is to come face-to-face with peoples and events of long ago through contemporary records. This chapter provides an opportunity for the reader to engage directly with a short document from the Viking Age. However valuable the work of modern scholars may be, such secondary sources always rest on direct experience and reassessment of the primary sources, contemporary materials relating to the topic in question. This chapter presents an opportunity to explore a primary source with as little mediation as possible.

The text we have chosen for this exercise was written in the early 860s by a monk of the monastery of Saint Philibert at Noirmoutier named Ermentarius. Viking attacks in the first third of the ninth century allegedly forced these monks to abandon their monastery on the tiny exposed island of Noirmoutier at the mouth of the Loire River in 836 and seek safety elsewhere (see chapter 1), initiating a long period of wandering from site to site that lasted until 875, when they finally settled at Tournus in Burgundy some 300 miles away.

Ermentarius's Latin account of the miracles and translations (transfer of relics from one location to another) of Saint Philibert is an important and oft-cited account of the terror and devastation wrought by the Northmen on the Frankish empire—but its value as an historical text has been disputed.

Ermentarius's text belongs to a category known as the translation, a subgenre of hagiography (holy writing, writings on holiness; the lives of saints) that developed from the ninth century. Texts such as this have been characterized as falling between purely literary saints' lives and historical forms of writing such as chronicles and annals, a factor that makes their use for historical purposes particularly challenging (Geary 1990, 9–10). Unsurprisingly, scholars have arrived at differing conclusions concerning the historicity of the account. Some have seen the text as evidence of the catastrophic impact of the Viking attacks upon religious communities in northern Francia in the ninth century, attacks that allegedly led to an exodus of churchmen and holy relics out of these areas (see Lifshitz 1995). Other scholars emphasize the language and rhetorical structure of the document and advise against taking it at face value, arguing that it represents an example of the way the Vikings were "othered" in ninth-century Frankish texts (Nelson 2003, 9–10). Still others have investigated the background to these accounts of migrations and translations and have concluded that the movement of relics like those of Saint Philibert out of northern France in the ninth and tenth centuries owed much less to Viking attacks than has been thought, and more to outside intervention from Frankish rulers who desired to control the relics (Lifshitz 1995).

With these remarks as general guidance, readers are encouraged to formulate their own opinions about the value of the text to the study of the Vikings. In particular, readers may wish to attempt to balance the relative merits of the document as a nearly contemporary account written by someone who had good access to oral and written sources against the fact that it represents what might be described as a "victim impact statement." Some specific questions for reflection or discussion are provided following the text, but readers are encouraged not to rely heavily upon these. They should be treated merely as a springboard for further inquiry.

★ ★ ★

Source: trans. D. Herlihy, *The History of Feudalism* (New York: Harper and Row, 1970), pp. 8–13; P.E. Dutton, *Carolingian Civilization: A Reader*, 2nd ed. (Peterborough, ON: Broadview, 2004), pp. 468–71.

FROM THE FIRST BOOK OF MIRACLES

We wish to describe the miracles which the most mighty and gracious God deigned to display when the body of the most blessed Philibert was taken from the ocean island known as Herius [Noirmoutier] to the place which used to be called Deé [St-Philibert de Grandlieu]. We want also to describe those deeds of heaven done in the same place, which we were present to see, or which we know to have been truthfully reported by the faithful. First, with all my strength I pray to the most powerful and gracious Lord, that He who deigned to display so many miracles by the merits of his confessor should grant also to me the eloquence to describe them.

But before I broach these things, I thought it valuable to explain the reason why [the saint] had to be taken from that place which he loved more than anywhere else and which also had seen him deliver his soul to God and his body to the earth. Although this may be well known to almost everyone alive, nevertheless, for the benefit of those to come, I shall state that in this affair the difficulty was the sudden and unforeseen attacks of the Northmen. When these men so often converged on the island's port and, being a fierce people, savagely devastated it, the inhabitants followed the example of their leader and sought help in flight rather than in waiting for their own extermination. The inhabitants moved back and forth in accord with the seasons. For in the summer, when the weather favored navigation, they sought the monastery of Deé, which had been built for this purpose, and only during the winter did they return to the island of Noirmoutier. Even as the monks and their dependents who inhabited the island were struggling in so desperate a situation, dangers began to multiply, and, for reason of the frequent raids of the Northmen, the people of the island began not only to be terrorized but to suffer the loss of their possessions and to be afflicted by extreme tribulations. But in truth this is what they feared most: that the faithless men would dig up the grave of the blessed Philibert and scatter whatever they found hither and yon, or rather throw it into the sea. This was known to have happened in the region of Brittany to the remains of certain holy men; this we were told by those who had seen it and had fled before the most oppressive rule of these men. Peace, however, will usually follow persecution; for the Lord does not abandon those who place their hopes in Him, as He says to his disciples: "Behold I am with you all days, even to the consummation of the world." Still, we must spend some time in explaining for what purpose the island was deprived of so great a patron and abandoned by the entire community of monks. Do not, however, wonder that I should have said that peace follows persecution. For in our mind no little peace was obtained when the most holy body was removed to a place where his servants, secure from barbarian attack, were allowed day and night to worship the Lord.

It was the year of the incarnation of the Lord and Redeemer Jesus Christ, 836, the fourteenth indiction, the twenty-third year in which the glorious emperor Louis [the Pious] was happily reining under the protection of divine mercy, and his son Lothar ruled in Italy, Pepin in Aquitaine, and Louis [the German] in Norica. The venerable abbot Hilbodus was governing, with the favor of the Lord, the flock of the confessor of Christ, Philibert, according to the Rule of Saint Benedict. At his command I, the most miserable of all his monks—not only in deeds, but also in words—assumed the task of telling these things. The frequent and unfortunate attacks of the Northmen, as has been said, were in no wise abating, and Abbot Hilbodus had built a castle on the island for protection against the faithless people. Together with the council of his brothers, he came to King Pepin [I, of Aquitaine] and asked his highness what he intended to do about this problem. Then the glorious king and the great men of the realm—a general assembly of the kingdom was then being held—deliberated concerning the problem with gracious concern and found themselves unable to help through mounting a vigorous assault. Because of the extremely dangerous tides, the island was not always readily accessible to our forces, while all knew that it was quite accessible to the Northmen whenever the sea was peaceful. The king and the great men chose what they believed to be the more advantageous policy. With the agreement of the most serene king Pepin, almost all the bishops of the province of Aquitaine, and the abbots, counts, and other faithful men who were present, and many others besides who had learned about the situation, unanimously advised that the body of the blessed Philibert ought to be taken from the island and no longer allowed to remain there. This decision was taken in the year of the Incarnation of our Lord Jesus Christ as was written above [836]. But enough! Now we shall turn our pen to describing his miracles....

FROM THE SECOND BOOK OF MIRACLES

In the preceding book I wrote, although less worthily than I should have, concerning the miracles of the blessed Philibert. Insofar as I had the time, I set forth the signs of his powers and described his splendid wonders. I had promised that I would in the following book recount those miracles omitted, or which divine power might further grant. Alas, I am forced to describe not miracles but the distressing troubles of nearly all the kingdom of the west. In order that my tale possess a logical order, I must explain the delays in time. This account was written for Hilduin [the abbot of St-Denis], who died some time back [in 842] and, as I had promised, for whoever might be interested in them. During the year of the Incarnation of Christ the Redeemer of all men, 836, a little peace smiled forth under the reign of Louis [the Pious], and amid the boundless joy of the people, as has been described, the body of the confessor was moved with solemn and universal honor, veneration, and glory. Not long thereafter, that is, four years later, the emperor died [in 840]. After a similar extent of time had passed, 67 ships of the Northmen suddenly attacked the valley of the Loire and captured the city of Nantes [in 843]. They put to the sword the bishop and his clergy together with a large multitude of the people; those who escaped death were delivered into slavery. The successor of the emperor Louis was Charles [the Bald], who had been raised in the royal palace. The brothers mentioned above—Lothar and Louis [the German], for Pepin had died before his father—each possessed his own kingdom. But since concise language is to be sought in such matters (for I did not begin this work to record deeds which were better left in silence, or better lamented, but to describe the miracles of the holy confessor), there first arose strife among the brothers, and finally among the chief persons of the realm. The younger brothers, Louis and Charles, rebelled against their older brother, Lothar. Wars, horrible as an intestinal disease, were heaped on wars. A sad and miserable victory fell to the younger brothers.

But their strife gave encouragement to the foreigners. Justice was abandoned, and evil advanced. No guards were mounted on the ocean beaches. Wars against foreign enemies ceased, and internal wars waged on. The number of ships grew larger, and the Northmen were beyond counting. Everywhere there were massacres of Christians, raids, devastations, and burnings. For as long as the world shall last, this will remain evident by the manifest signs. Whatever cities the Northmen attacked, they captured without resistance: Bordeaux, Périgueux, Saintes, Limoges, Angoulême, and Toulouse; then Angers, Tours, and Orléans were destroyed. The remains of numerous saints were carried off. What the Lord warns through the prophet came close to fulfillment: "From the north shall an evil break forth upon all the inhabitants of the land." We also fled to a place which is called Cunauld, in the territory of Anjou, on the banks of the Loire, which the glorious King Charles had given to us for the sake of refuge, because of the imminent peril, before Angers was taken. The body of the blessed Philibert still remained in the monastery which is called Deé, although that place had been burned by the Northmen. For it was not permitted that the banks of the Herbauge River should have been deprived of so great a patron, so long as some few of the monks were able to remain there.

Then, a few years later, an almost immeasurable fleet of Norse ships sailed up the Seine river. The evil done in those regions was no less than that perpetrated elsewhere. The Northmen attacked the city of Rouen and devastated and burned it [in 856–857]. They then captured Paris, Beauvais, and Meaux, and they also leveled the castle of Melun. Chartres was also taken. They struck into the cities of Evreux, Bayeux, and other neighboring towns. Almost no place, and no monastery, remained unscathed. Everyone gave himself over to flight; rare was the man who said: "Stay, stay, resist, fight for the fatherland, for children and relatives." Thus, losing heart and feuding among themselves, they purchased by tribute what they should have defended with arms, and the kingdom of the Christians succumbed.

The Northmen attacked Spain; they entered the Rhône River, and they devastated Italy. While everywhere so many domestic and foreign wars were raging, the year of the Incarnation of Christ 857 passed. As long as there had been in us some hope of returning to our own possessions (which, however, proved to be fruitless), the body of the blessed Philibert, as has been said, was left in his own soil. But since a refuge was nowhere to be found, we did not permit the most holy body to be carried with us hither and yon. Now, it was more truly smuggled away from the grasp of the Northmen than carried with festive praises, and it was taken to the place we have mentioned, which is called Cunauld. This was done in such a way that, when necessity required, it might be moved elsewhere. The year of the Lord's Incarnation was 862 the body was carried from Cunauld to Messay. It will later be evident how many miracles were shown forth in that place through his glorious merits. But first we shall describe those wonders which we omitted at the end of the preceding book. For just as the persecution of the pagans has not ceased, neither does time know how to stay its course; since the days menace me with their quick passing, already the hour and the circumstances require that I declare the miracles....

Questions

How does the author view the Northmen? How does he describe them?

What impact did the Northmen have on the Carolingian empire according to this account?

What impact did the Northmen have on monasteries according to this account?

How effective were the Carolingian rulers at responding to Viking attacks according to this account?

To what extent might the account exaggerate Norse atrocities?

AFTERWORD: VIKING IMPACTS AND LEGACIES

Between about 800 and 1100, the people known as the Vikings raided, traded, settled, explored, farmed, fished, and whaled from North America to the Middle East, interacting with an astonishing array of peoples along the way, from the Dorset and Thule cultures of the eastern Arctic to Greek-speaking Byzantines, and Arabs from the Middle East to the Iberian Peninsula. The chronological sweep of the Viking Age, its wide geographical reach, and its complexity combine to make evaluation of the period difficult. But what might a balance sheet of the Viking impact on early medieval Europe look like? And what legacies did they leave behind?

The impact of the Vikings has generally been seen as destructive, with the Vikings cast in the role of early medieval terrorists. Even allowing for the biases and exaggerations of early medieval sources, this view has much to commend it. Viking raids inflicted terror, shock, and awe on early medieval populations, and there can be no doubt that being on the receiving end of a Viking raid was a horrifying experience. Unsurprisingly, flight was a common response: many terrified monks abandoned their monasteries on exposed coastal locations; some of them never returned. Gaps in lists of bishops for many dioceses across Britain and Europe suggest further disruption of organized religion. Since churches and monasteries represented centers of learning and repositories of documents, raids on these places had broad implications. King Alfred, for instance, lamented the decline of learning brought about by the ravages of the Northmen. Viking disrespect for ecclesiastical centers may even have influenced the behavior of the locals: some studies suggest an increase in violence directed toward churches and monasteries on the part of local populations during the Viking Age. Still other groups may have deliberately "gone Norse" and adopted aspects of Viking culture: this is one interpretation of the mysterious group known as the "Foreigner Gaels" mentioned in some ninth-century Irish sources who harassed Irish, Scots, and Scandinavians alike. All of this, of course, must be viewed against the backdrop of an early medieval Europe in which violence was commonplace and few people lived in anything approaching security.

Assessing the economic impact of Viking raiding is more difficult still. Towns and trading centers were attacked. Some of them, such as Dorestad, an important Carolingian trading center, subsequently disappeared entirely. But the question of Viking responsibility for the destruction of Dorestad is a vexed one: modern scholarship attributes its decay not to the Vikings so much as to environmental factors.

Even if Viking attacks are now believed to have played a less significant role in the break-up of the Carolingian empire than was once thought (internecine strife among the ruling dynasties is now considered more significant), Viking conquest and settlement indeed disrupted existing power structures across Europe and the British Isles. The ravages of the Great Army in England eliminated several Anglo-Saxon kingdoms in little more than a decade, clearing the way for the rise of a unified England under the descendants of King Alfred. Viking raiding and settlement may have annihilated the indigenous Pictish population in the northern islands of Orkney and Shetland; whether that is the case or not, the islands and their inhabitants became Scandinavian in speech and culture. Viking activity may also have played a role in weakening the Picts and facilitating the movement of the Gaelic-speaking Scots of Dalriada into eastern Scotland, following which the Picts disappear from historical records. The Vikings therefore contributed substantially to the making of the medieval kingdoms of England and Scotland.

Scandinavian settlement on the Continent was less extensive but produced equally profound results. The settlement of Scandinavians at the mouth of the Seine River in the early tenth century created the duchy of Normandy, and although the Scandinavians who settled here soon became French in language and culture, they did not forget their Scandinavian roots as they embarked on their own eleventh-century diaspora that included conquests in southern Italy, Sicily, and England. Scandinavian influence in eastern Europe is a much contested topic in Viking studies: for years scholars have debated what role the Rūs played in the establishment of Russia, a country to which they gave its name.

The Vikings also created realms in Scandinavia. The medieval kingdoms of Denmark, Norway, and Sweden that emerged during the Viking Age as localized chiefdoms coalesced into unified kingdoms under ambitious and often ruthless Viking rulers. If the Viking Age site at Jelling in the Jutland peninsula in Denmark is justly referred to as the "birth certificate of Denmark," the Vikings by extension wrote the birth certificates of medieval Scandinavia.

Viking settlement brought further social and economic change. To early medieval Ireland, entirely devoid of urban centers, the Vikings introduced towns and important trading centers; their influence here was out of all proportion to the extent of settlement. Dublin, Waterford, Wexford, and Cork owe their origins to Viking settlements. Viking merchants created trade networks that stretched from Kiev and Novgorod to York and Dublin, and from Constantinople to Greenland. Thousands of Islamic silver coins found in Swedish archaeological sites are the result of trade, not plunder. Viking merchants have been described as early capitalists and savvy marketers. The terms may be modern ones, but the Vikings were certainly shrewd businessmen. The thirteenth-century Norwegian text *The King's Mirror* is a sort of Vikings' guide to good business. Set in the form of a dialogue between a father and son, all sorts of useful business advice is offered that resonates through the ages:

> If you are staying in market towns...and you don't know how buying and selling is done there, observe carefully how those who are reputed to be the best and most successful merchants carry on their trading. When you are buying, take a careful look at the merchandise before clinching the deal, in case it is damaged or flawed in any way. And whenever you seal a bargain, always have a few trustworthy men present to witness the transaction....

Colonization of the North Atlantic islands of the Faeroes, Iceland, and Greenland occurred without disruption to existing populations, since these islands were largely uninhabited (with the exception of a few Irish hermits who promptly left when the Norse arrived). The Norse discovery and reconnaissance of these islands is testament to the role of the Scandinavians as explorers and great seafarers. The colonization of the Faeroes, Iceland, and Greenland and the establishment of new societies there is one of the great achievements of the Viking Age. The Viking legacy survives in modern Faeroese and Icelandic DNA, language, and culture. Greenland is often described as a "failed" colony, but it is worth bearing in mind that a Norse presence endured there for the same period of time that separates us from the first European settlers in the New World. Viking voyages to North America are sometimes described as a failed experiment, but this is not entirely accurate. They symbolize the reach, drive, and ambition of the Vikings, and it is evident that Norse Greenlanders continued making voyages to North America in search of resources for centuries after the few voyages described in saga accounts. In global terms, the Norse voyages to North America represent the closing of the circle of human contact between Europe and the Americas.

Ships made the voyages possible, and the Viking ship has justly been called the northern counterpart of the Parthenon. A visit to the ship museums in Oslo and Roskilde confirms that assessment. Like the Parthenon, the surviving Viking ships offer visual and tactile links to a lost age of considerable aesthetic sophistication and technological genius. The Vikings made a huge contribution to the design and development of the ship. Viking ships were built from wood, and Viking domestic architecture used the same material. Olaf the Peacock's fine paneling and tapestries at Hjardarholt have all vanished, except in the poetry of Ulfr Uggason. Viking Age craftsmanship in wood and metal is celebrated by Bragi Boddason's *Ragnarsdrápa*, as well as surviving in considerable quantities in archaeological finds from across the reach of the Viking world.

The baroque magnificence of skaldic poetry and the enduring narratives of *The Poetic Edda* form a lasting monument. The sagas of Icelanders are unrivaled in medieval narrative and present the thirteenth century's memory of an age and ideology already belonging to the past when the saga manuscripts were written down. It is not a stretch to see these sagas as the first historical novels. In addition, the gods and goddesses of Northern Europe have never really gone away; sagas recount occasional visitations by ousted gods to reproach their former followers. From the eighteenth century onwards, scholars, poets, and novelists have rediscovered what the Icelanders never forgot. Writers as different as J.R.R. Tolkien and Halldor Laxness (see his *Gerpla*) continue to provide evidence of the imaginative force of the early narratives. Norse mythology has played a powerful part in some of the best—and worst—moments of European cultural history.

Assemblies are another legacy of the Vikings. The Icelandic parliament, the Althing, established by Norse settlers in 930, celebrated its millennial anniversary in 1930. The place-name Tynwald in the Isle of Man commemorates a Norse assembly in the island. The modern Manx parliament retains the name, and once a year, on Tynwald Day (the Manx national holiday), 5 July, an open-air assembly is held on the site. It is an enduring monument to the Norse heritage of the island.

In linguistic terms, Old Norse was a strong influence on the transition from Anglo-Saxon to Middle English. Those parts of England most heavily settled by Norsemen lost the older inflectional system much earlier than other parts of the country. Though not caused by Norse influence alone, this important process was certainly accelerated by their presence. The imposition of pronouns by one language on another is unusual, but English now uses the historically Norse *they, them,* and *their* instead of the Anglo-Saxon *hie, hem,* and *heora.* Some have suggested that borrowing of this intimacy argues that the two languages had merged, forming a *creole.* While few scholars are willing to go so far, the borrowing of pronouns and a large commonplace vocabulary do suggest a very intimate contact with enduring effects. Old Norse loans in English are surprising in that they are largely unneeded, though borrowing generally expresses some felt cultural need (similar, for instance, to French culinary terms in the modern period). Norsemen probably brought the words into English as their own language came to be used less and less in England. Among the many nouns we owe to the Norse is this random group: *skin, skirt, sky, egg, loan, dirt, dregs,* and *keel.* A sampling of verbs: *glitter, kindle, raise,* and *ransack*. English place names ending in *−by* (*Grimsby*, *Derby*, etc.) and *−thorp(e)* (*Althorp*, *Gawsthorpe*, etc.) are reminders that Norsemen settled there. That the English language borrowed the Norse word *law* (ON *lög*) reminds us that a Scandinavian legal system, brought by Viking Age settlers, was a force for order and civility in much of Anglo-Saxon England.

★ ★ ★

The age to which the Vikings have given their name was a complex and multi-faceted period. The Vikings unquestionably brought terror and destruction to large parts of Europe, but their footprint was more enduring and more signifi-cant than that. The Viking Age was a remarkable period in European history, and the Vikings continue to capture and excite our imagination.

QUESTIONS FOR REFLECTION

What is meant by the word "Viking"? How has the meaning of the word changed over time?

What was the Viking Age, and what types of activity characterized it?

Is the term Viking *Age* adequate, or should we think in terms of Viking *Ages*?

How different were the Vikings from their European contemporaries?

With reference to the discussion in chapter 1 on the Vikings in the courtroom of history, which interpretation of the Vikings do you favor, and why?

What range of sources would an historian of the Viking Age employ?

How does the nature of the surviving source material shape and influence our understanding of the Vikings?

Do sources vary in trustworthiness? Why? How?

What impact did the Vikings have on early medieval society?

How far do you agree or disagree with the assessment of the Vikings in the afterword?

What was the influence of the Viking Age on the culture of modern Europe?

What, if anything, has changed in your estimation of the Vikings after reading this book?

CHRONOLOGY

The chronology is not comprehensive and reflects only people and events mentioned in the text.

SCANDINAVIAN HOMELANDS

Denmark

ca 737	Construction of the Danevirke
ca 750–800	origins of Birka, Ribe, Kaupang, Hedeby
810	death of Godfred king of Danes
810–857	dynastic struggles among Godfred's kin
826	Danish king Harald Klak baptized at Mainz

Jelling dynasty

ca 936–958	Gorm the Old
958–987	Harald Bluetooth
	ca 965: Conversion of Harald Bluetooth, king of Denmark
	ca 965–980s: Harald Bluetooth erects Jelling monuments in Jutland
	ca 980s: fortifications at Trelleborg constructed by Harald Bluetooth
987–1014	Svein Forkbeard
	1013: Danish conquest of England
1019–35	Cnut the Great (king of England, 1016)
1035–42	Harthacnut
1042–46	Magnus the Good (king of Norway, 1035)

Norway

834	Oseberg ship burial
ca 880–930	Harald Finehair
	ca 885–900: battle of Hafsfjord
ca 900	Gokstad ship burial

ca 930–936	Eirik Bloodax (king of York, 947–48, 952–54)
ca 936–960	Hakon I the Good
ca 960–970	Harald Greycloak
995–1000	Olaf Tryggvasson
1000	battle of Svöld
1015–1030	Olaf Haraldsson (Saint Olaf)
	1030: battle of Sticklestad
1035–46	Magnus the Good
1047–66	Harald Hardradi

Sweden

| 995–1022 | Olof Skötkonung |

BRITAIN AND IRELAND

789	Northmen land near Portland and kill king's representative
793	raid on Lindisfarne
795	Vikings in Hebrides and Irish Sea
806	68 monks of Iona slain
825	Iona attacked; the monk Blathmac slain
837	large fleets on Liffey and Boyne in Ireland
839–840	first overwintering in Ireland
841	naval base (*longphort*) established at Dublin
850	first overwintering in England, on Thanet
ca 850	settlement in Orkney and Shetland islands
851	conflict among different Viking groups for control of Dublin
852	first recorded raid on Wales
865	arrival of Danish Great Army in England
866	Great Army captures York; establishment of Viking kingdom of York
870	East Anglia overrun by Danes; King Edmund slain
871–899	Alfred the Great, king of Wessex
873–874	Great Army winters at Repton and drives out king of Mercia
878	King Alfred defeats Gunthrum at battle of Edington; treaty of Wedmore; establishment of the Danelaw
ca 900	settlement in the Isle of Man
ca 900	earldom of Orkney established
902	Irish temporarily force Vikings out of Dublin
902–954	English reconquer Danelaw territories

917	Norse retake Dublin
937	battle of Brunanburh, England: King Athelstan defeats a coalition of Norse and Scots
ca 947–48	Eirik Bloodax, king of York
ca 952–54	Eirik Bloodax, king of York
978–1016	Athelred II, king of England
980	renewed Viking attacks on England
991	battle of Maldon; English pay 10,000 lb of silver to buy off raiders
994	English pay 16,000 lb of silver
1002	Saint Brice's Day massacre
1013	Svein Forkbeard, king of Denmark, conquers England
1014	death of Svein Forkbeard
1014–1016	struggle between Danes and English for control of England
1014	battle of Clontarf, Ireland
1016	Cnut conquers England
ca 1042	Skuldelev 2 longship constructed from timber felled in eastern Ireland
1042	Danish rule in England ends
1066	battles of Stamford Bridge and Hastings
1098	Magnus Barelegs' royal expedition through Hebrides
1103	Magnus Barelegs slain in Ireland
1116/17	death of Magnus Erlendsson (Saint Magnus of Orkney)
1171	English conquest of Dublin

WESTERN EUROPE

768–814	Charlemagne, king of Franks
799	first recorded raid on Continent
800	Charlemagne organizes naval defenses against North Sea pirates
804–810	Godfred, king of Danes, active on frontiers of Frankish kingdom
810	Frisian coast attacked
814–840	Louis the Pious, king of Franks
826	Harald Klak, king of Denmark, baptized at Mainz
826–829	Saint Anskar's Christian missions to Denmark and Sweden
834–837	attacks on Dorestad (important Carolingian trading center)
842	Quentovic sacked; first overwintering in Francia
843	Treaty of Verdun; partition of Carolingian empire
840–877	Charles the Bald, king of West Franks

843	Nantes sacked; Viking base established at mouth of Loire
844	first raid on Spain (Seville)
845	attack on Paris; first tribute paid by Franks
846–847	raids on Brittany
859–862	raids in Mediterranean by Hastein and Bjorn Ironside
860	Pisa, Luna, and Fiesole in Italy sacked
860	Viking chieftain Weland hired by Frankish king to attack Seine Vikings
862	fortified bridge at Pîtres on the Seine begun
865	Saint Anskar dies
885–886	siege of Paris
ca 911	Normandy granted to Rollo/Hrolf
914–919	Brittany occupied by Vikings
931–939	reconquest of Brittany by Bretons
960s	raids on Galicia, Spain

THE EAST

ca 750–800	Scandinavians at Staraya Ladoga
838/39	Swedes (Rūs) at Constantinople
860	Constantinople attacked for first time
ca 862	Rurik established at Novgorod
ca 882	Novgorod and Kiev united
907	attack on Constantinople; trade treaty between Rūs and Byzantines
911	attack on Constantinople; trade treaty
912	Scandinavian raiders on Caspian Sea
922	Ibn Fadlan, an Arab diplomat, meets Rūs on the Volga
941	attack on Constantinople; treaty with Byzantines
ca 950–1000	establishment of Varangian guard at Constantinople
987	Scandinavian raids in Caucasus region (also 989, 1030, 1032)
ca 1040	Ingvar's expedition to Serkland

NORTH ATLANTIC

ca 825	Irish hermits driven out of Faeroe Islands by Vikings
ca 825–870	Iceland sighted and explored
871–930	settlement of Iceland (the Settlement Age)
930	establishment of Althing in Iceland
ca 982–985	Eirik Thorvaldsson the Red explores Greenland
ca 985–986	settlement of Greenland begins

ca 985–986	Bjarni Herjolfsson sights lands west of Greenland
999–1000	conversion of Iceland
ca 1000	Leif Eiriksson explores Vínland
ca 1000–20	voyages to Vínland; site at L'Anse aux Meadows (Newfoundland) in use
1056	first bishopric established at Skalholt in Iceland
1122	bishopric established at Gardar in Greenland

GLOSSARY

Althing: the Icelandic national assembly (established 930) and held for two weeks annually around midsummer at Thingvellir.

Anglo-Saxons: term for the Germanic peoples who settled in Britain from the fifth century, including Angles, Saxons, Frisians, and Jutes. The Anglo-Saxon era in English history is considered as ca 500–1066.

Anglo-Saxon Chronicle: term applied to a group of manuscripts that record English history from 60 BCE to 1154 CE. Begun in the reign of King Alfred of Wessex (r. 871–899), the *Chronicle* is an important source for Viking activities in England.

Annal: brief record of yearly events in chronological order, originating in the need to calculate the correct date for the celebration of Easter, the most important festival in the Christian ritual year. Annals typically lack analysis, explanation, or interpretation.

Asgard (*Ásgarðr*): the dwelling place of the gods. The word *garðr* means *yard, enclosed space. See also* Midgard; Utgard.

Æsir: main group of the Norse gods, as opposed to the Vanir (see below) with whom they fought a war. *Æsir* is plural; the singular is *áss*. The etymology of *áss* is uncertain; it may be descended from an Indo-European word meaning *breath* or be related to terms meaning *binding* or *controlling*. Snorri Sturluson historicizes or euhemerizes the Æsir by deriving their name from *Asia*. His *Prose Edda* treats them as an Asiatic tribe with magical powers.

Berserkers: ferocious warriors who worked themselves into a frenzy (*berserksgangr*) and fought without regard for their safety in the belief that they could not be harmed by weapons. Berserkers were particularly associated with the god Odin, and with shape-shifting, and one etymology for the word proposes that it is derived from *bear* + *serk* (*shirt*), meaning one who wears a bear skin.

Book prose theory and free prose theory: conflicting theories of the origin of *The Sagas of Icelanders*. Book prose theory regards the sagas as the literary productions of authors writing within a manuscript tradition. Free prose theory considers that the sagas had oral roots and may have attained a sophisticated oral form before being written down in the thirteenth and fourteenth centuries.

Booth(s) (*buð*; pl. *buðir*): temporary dwellings used at assemblies and other seasonally occupied sites with permanent walls that were probably covered with a tent-like roof of cloth.

Byzantine empire: the Eastern Roman Empire of Late Antiquity and the Middle Ages, centered on the city of Constantinople (Byzantium), modern-day Istanbul in Turkey; *see* Mikligarðr.

Carolingian empire: territory in western Europe ruled by the family of Charlemagne (r. 768–814); it reached its greatest extent under Charlemagne but divided into western, middle, and eastern kingdoms in 843.

Carolingians: the family of Frankish aristocrats and the dynasty they established that ruled much of western Europe between ca 750 and 887.

Chronicle: common form of historical writing in the European Middle Ages, closely related to, and sometimes overlapping with, annals and histories; typically organized chronologically.

Contemporary sagas (*Samtíðarsögur, Samtímasögur*): these were nearly contemporary with the events they narrate, mainly in late twelfth- and thirteenth-century Iceland, the Age of the Sturlungs (*Sturlungaöld*).

Dalriada: kingdom established in the west of Scotland ca 500 by Gaelic speaking Scoti from Ireland.

Danegeld: tribute paid to Danish Vikings in England and elsewhere in western Europe to buy off further attacks.

Danelaw: the part of northern and eastern England settled by the Danes in the late ninth century and influenced by Danish customs.

Danevirke: series of ramparts and ditches along the southern border of medieval Denmark at the base of the Jutland peninsula, stretching some 30 km and built at various times. The earliest phase dates from 737, with many subsequent expansions and reconstructions.

Dendrochronology: tree-ring dating, which utilizes the size and pattern of tree-rings to date timber artifacts by matching them against sequences of tree-rings for a particular region.

Earl (*jarl* [ON]): title of men of high rank, either independent rulers or subordinate to kings.

Franks: Germanic people originating in the lower/mid-Rhine region in the third century who expanded westward and, following the collapse of the Western Roman Empire in the fifth century, created a kingdom that extended over most of modern France and parts of western Germany and the Low Countries. Established by Clovis (d. 511), the Frankish kingdom lasted until the Treaty of Verdun (843), when it was divided among the sons of Louis the Pious (d. 840).

Free prose theory: *see under* book prose theory

Germanic: a westerly branch of the Indo-European language family. The Scandinavian languages constitute the northern branch of Germanic.

Godi (*goði*; pl. *goðar*): until 1263, an Icelandic local chieftain; prominent settlers in Iceland established themselves as chieftains and distributed land among their followers. *Godis* were responsible for carrying out the business of government and the administration of justice at local assemblies (Things) and at the Althing. The *godi's* authority rested on his ability to safeguard the interests of his supporters (thingmen) who were free to vote with their feet if the *godi* proved inadequate.

Götar: at the start of the Viking Age, one of several peoples in modern-day Sweden, inhabiting the Östergötland and Västergötland regions.

Great Army: Viking army of Danish origin that invaded England in 865 under several leaders, including the sons of the semi-legendary Danish King Ragnar Loðbrók ("Hairy-Breeches"). Its conquests significantly altered the political geography of England. Its size is disputed; it may have numbered in the thousands, and it probably comprised the warbands of a number of different kings and chieftains.

Hagiography: genre of medieval literature concerned with the lives of saints; sacred biography.

Hebrides: islands off the west coast of Scotland that were settled by Scandinavians from the middle of the ninth century, becoming known to Gaelic speakers as *Innse Gall*, "the Isles of the Foreigners."

Icelandic Commonwealth: the period of Icelandic history between the establishment of the national assembly (the Althing) in 930 and the establishment of Norwegian hegemony over the island in 1263.

Iron Age: The final phase of prehistory in Europe, following the Bronze Age, and characterized by iron-working technology ca 1000 BCE–500 CE. In Scandinavia the Iron Age begins ca 500 BCE and extends to the Viking Age (ca 800).

Kings' sagas (*Konungasögur*): biographies of Scandinavian kings from mythological prehistory until the thirteenth century. Most were written in Iceland or recorded in Icelandic manuscripts.

Knörr: a merchant vessel.

Legendary sagas (*Fornaldarsögur*): sagas set in the old world before the Saga Age (before ca 870) and inhabited by trolls, giants, dwarves, and ferocious kings.

Longphort: naval encampment used by the Vikings in ninth-century Ireland for their first overwinterings. Dublin's origins lie in a *longphort*, though its exact location remains uncertain.

Longship (*langskip*): a large warship.

Medieval Warm Period (Medieval Climatic Optimum; Little Climatic Optimum): a period of warmer climatic conditions than those prevailing previously or afterwards, in Europe and the North Atlantic, ca 950 to 1250. Temperatures in the North Atlantic may have been as much as 4°C warmer than those prevailing in the mid-twentieth century. It was followed by a climatic downturn known as the Little Ice Age, ca 1350–1850.

Midgard (*Miðgarðr*): the middle-enclosure, middle-earth, the home of mankind.

Mikligarðr: Old Norse term for Byzantium/Constantinople, capital of the Eastern Roman Empire. It means "the great city."

Niflheim: the Land of Mists is the underworld residence of the dead, ruled over by the goddess Hel, daughter of Loki. Hel will lead the dead from her residence to fight against the gods at Ragnarök.

Old Norse: belongs to the Germanic group of Indo-European languages. Old Norse was the northerly form of Germanic as spoken in Scandinavia and areas of Scandinavian settlement. Runic inscriptions in early Old Norse survive from the second century. By ca 1000, Old Norse was evolving into the modern Scandinavian languages. Modern Icelandic has remained closest in form to Old Norse.

Picts: the indigenous people of northern Scotland at the time of the Viking expansion. The Scots of Dalriada conquered or assimilated the Picts from the mid-ninth century.

The Poetic Edda (*The Elder Edda*): this term is applied to the surviving body of Old Norse heroic and mythological poetry. Most of it is contained in one thirteenth-century Icelandic manuscript, the Codex Regius, which is preserved in the Arni Magnusson Institute in Reykjavík.

The Prose Edda (*The Younger Edda* or *Snorra Edda [Snorri's Edda]*): written by Snorri Sturluson in the first half of the thirteenth century, this work is an art of skaldic poetry. In the first part, *The Deception of Gylfi* (*Gylfaginning*), Snorri recounts many of the myths from which skaldic poetry drew its figurative language. The second part, *Skáldskaparmál* (*Poetic Diction*) contains a collection of skaldic verses with Snorri's commentary. In part 3, *List of Meters* (*Háttatal*), Snorri gives his own examples of the various metrical forms used by skalds. The term *edda* probably means "compositions."

Ragnarök (*Ragnarökr*): generally translated as the *Twilight of the Gods*. In a last great battle, the giants, Loki and his offspring, and the inhabitants of Niflheim will destroy the gods and themselves. The details of the battle are the material of Norse prophetic literature such as *The Prophecy of the Seeress* (*Völuspá*). The poem ends with the prophecy of the emergence of a brave new world with the resurrection of Baldur, Odin's long dead son.

Runes: the letters of the *futhark*, a script based on northern Italian scripts. The name *futhark* is made up of the first six letters of the script. Runes were thought to have a magical significance. Egil Skallagrimsson, for instance, inscribes runes on a drinking horn to counteract the effects of poisoned beer.

Rūs: term used in western and eastern sources to denote Scandinavian traders, mercenaries, and adventurers venturing along the routes from the Baltic Sea down the Russian river systems to Constantinople and Baghdad.

Saga: a type of prose narrative written in Old Norse, produced mainly in Iceland from the late twelfth until the fourteenth century. *Saga* (pl. *sögur*) is related to *segja* (*to say, tell, report*), and its root meaning is "something said, or narrated orally: a story."

Sagas of Icelanders: formerly known as *Family Sagas*, these offer accounts of the settlement and later history of Iceland during what is termed the Saga Age, from ca 870 until ca 1030, shortly after the conversion of Iceland. The sagas focus on the exploits of particular heroes (e.g., *Egil's Saga*) or on the history of prominent families (*The Saga of the People of Laxardale*).

Sami: the indigenous peoples of northern Scandinavia, including northern Norway, Sweden, and Finland, as well as the Kola Peninsula in Russia, speakers of a non-Germanic Finno-Ugric language.

Scots: Gaelic-speaking Irish immigrants who established the kingdom of Dalriada on the west coast of Scotland ca 500. Throughout the early Middle Ages the term referred to both the inhabitants of Ireland and the kingdom of Dalriada.

Serkland: Old Norse term used for areas under Islamic control in the Middle East.

Settlement Age: the period in Icelandic history during which the Norse settled the island, roughly 870 to the establishment of the Althing in 930.

Skaldic poetry: also known as Poetry of the *Drótt*, or court, and first composed in Norway in the ninth century, it reached its maturity in Iceland from the early tenth century. Skaldic poets were chiefly court poets. The term *skáld* may be related to the English *scold*, perhaps an indication of satirical origins. Skaldic poetry ceased to be composed in the fourteenth century.

Snorri Sturluson (ca 1179–23 September 1241): the most important of medieval Icelandic writers. His major works are *Heimskringla* (*The Lives of the Kings of Norway*) and *The Prose Edda*. He is also regarded as the probable author of *Egil's Saga*. Snorri belonged to the Sturlung family, which dominated Icelandic politics in the early thirteenth century. He was elected Lawspeaker three times and was deeply involved with Icelandic politics. He took the wrong side in a dispute with King Hakon the Old of Norway and was assassinated at his home in Reykjaholt, Iceland.

Svear: inhabitants of the Uppland region of modern-day central Sweden, with an important center at Uppsala. The Svear gave their name to Sweden.

Þáttr (pl. þættir): literally, this term means a single strand of a rope and is extended to mean a section of a text. The term is also applied to short narratives included in more extensive sagas. Typically in a *þáttr*, an Icelander arrives at a foreign court (frequently, the Norwegian court) and distinguishes himself by his talents or character.

Thing (þing): Old Norse term for an assembly. Assemblies were held at local and regional levels across the Scandinavian world; the Althing in Iceland (est. 930) was the only national assembly. Free adult men were the main participants; women participated occasionally and children and slaves not at all. Things met at specific sites at regular intervals for many purposes, and also played a role in king-making. One of the most famous regional assemblies was the Gulathing in Norway.

Utgard (Útgarðar, Snorri's form is plural: The Outer Lands, or Area): the home of the giants. The home of the giants lies beyond the sea that encircles Midgard. In this sea dwells the World-Serpent (*Miðgarðsormr, Jörmungandr*). Utgard is also known as *Jötunheim* (sometimes *Jötunheimar* [pl.]); *Jötun* means *giant*.

Valhalla (Valhöll): the Hall of the Slain, Odin's residence. According to Snorri (in *Gylfaginning*), his chosen warriors (*einherjar*) feasted there by night and fought by day until they were needed for the last battle against the giants and monsters at Ragnarök. The *val* element of the word may signify *splendid*.

Valkyries: lit. "choosers of the slain," maidens who ferried the souls of Odin's chosen warriors (*einherjar*) to Valhalla. They are sometimes shown serving drink in Valhalla. In some sources they appear to be divine beings, in others they are mortal women. Perhaps the best known is Brynhild, daughter of Budli, betrothed to Sigurd, but treacherously married to Gunnar.

Vanir: a tribe of gods who came into conflict with the Æsir, by whom they were finally absorbed. The Vanir are sometimes regarded as fertility gods who succumbed to a more aggressive group. Njörd, Freyn, Freyja, and Kvasir are identified as Vanir. Freyn and Freyja, brother and sister, were Njörd's offspring by his sister; incest appears to have been acceptable among the Vanir.

Varangians: Scandinavians in the eastern Mediterranean, as well as Scandinavian mercenaries in the service of the Byzantine emperors, especially members of the Varangian Guard, an elite corps within the Byzantine army comprised of Scandinavians and, after 1066, Anglo-Saxons.

Viking (víkingr): one who takes part in a *víking*, a piratical expedition. The word is now generally applied to Scandinavians who lived during the Viking Age and to their culture. One view derives the word from ON *vík*, meaning *bay*. Vikings would then be haunters of bays from which they carried out raids. Another possibility is that the place name Víken (the Oslo Fjord district of Norway) is the source of the word. The most recent suggestion relates *víkingr* to the ON noun *vika*, a unit of rowing distance at which rowers changed shifts, a view supported by the existence of the ON verb *víkja, to move aside, give way.*

Viking Age: period of European and particularly Scandinavian history that is generally considered to begin with the onset of Scandinavian raiding activity around 800. There is less certainty about when it ended, but a date of ca 1100 is commonly accepted.

Vínland: lit. "Wine Land," so named for grape vines found in the region. Along with Helluland ("Slab-rock Land") and Markland ("Forest Land"), one of the regions on the east coast of North America visited by Scandinavians ca 1000. Current thinking suggests Helluland is Baffin Island, Markland is Labrador, and the Gulf of St. Lawrence region is Vínland, though the location of the latter has engendered much debate.

The War between the Æsir and the Vanir: this is the first war. It is mentioned in *The Prophecy of the Seeress* and in Snorri's *Heimskringla* and *Edda*. While it is not clear that either side won a decisive victory, the Vanir appear to be absorbed by the Æsir.

Yggdrasil: the World Tree, which stands at the center of the universe. Its roots extend to the inhabited worlds. *The Sayings of the High One (Hávamál)* relates that Odin hung on a tree for nine days and nights and thus gained the wisdom of the runes. Since *Ygg-* (= terror) is a synonym for Odin and *drasill* means horse, it is assumed that he suffered on Yggdrasil.

REFERENCES

Andersson, T. 1967. *The Icelandic Family Saga: an analytic reading*. Cambridge, MA: Harvard University Press.

Andersson, T. 2006. *The Growth of the Medieval Icelandic Sagas (1180–1280)*. Ithaca, NY, & London: Cornell University Press.

Barrett, J.H. 2008. "What Caused the Viking Age?" *Antiquity* 82: 671–85.

Brooks, N.P. 1979. "England in the Ninth Century: the crucible of defeat." *Transactions of the Royal Historical Society* 29: 1–20. http://dx.doi.org/10.2307/3679110.

Clark, K. 1969. *Civilisation: a personal view*. New York & London: Harper & Row.

Clover, C.J. 1982. *The Medieval Saga*. Ithaca, NY, & London: Cornell University Press.

Clunies Ross, M. (ed.) 2008. *Skaldic Poetry of the Scandinavian Middle Ages (SKALD 7). Poetry on Christian subjects*. 2 vols. Turnout: Brepols.

Coupland, S. 2003. "The Vikings on the Continent in Myth and History." *History* 88 (290): 186–203. http://dx.doi.org/10.1111/1468-229X.00258.

Cusack, C. 1998. *The Rise of Christianity in Northern Europe, 300–1000*. London & New York: Cassell.

Dennis, A., P. Foote, & R. Perkins, ed. & trans. 2000. *Laws of Early Iceland. Grágas II*. Winnipeg: University of Manitoba Press.

Dumville, D. 1997. *The Churches of North Britain in the First Viking-Age*. Fifth Whithorn Lecture. Whithorn: Friends of the Whithorn Trust.

Dumville, D. 2008. "Vikings in Insular Chronicling." In *The Viking World*, ed. S. Brink in collaboration with N. Price, 350–67. London & New York: Routledge.

Earl, J.W. 1999. "Violence and Non-Violence in Anglo-Saxon England: Aelfric's 'Passion of St. Edmund.'" *Philological Quarterly* 78 (1/2): 125–49.

Einarsson, Bjarni, ed. 2003. *Egils Saga*. London: Viking Society for Northern Research.

Fletcher, R. 1998. *The Barbarian Conversion: from paganism to Christianity*. New York: H. Holt and Co.

Foot, S. 1991. "Violence against Christians? The Vikings and the church in ninth-century England." *Medieval History* 1 (3): 3–16.

Foote, P.G., and D.M. Wilson. 1970. *The Viking Achievement: the society and culture of early medieval Scandinavia.* Sidgwick & Jackson Great Civilizations Series. London: Sidgwick & Jackson.

Gade, K.E. (ed.). 2009. *Skaldic Poetry of the Scandinavian Middle Ages (SKALD 2). Poetry from the King's Sagas 2.* Turnout: Brepols.

Geary, P.J. 1990. *Furta Sacra: thefts of relics in the central Middle Ages.* Rev. ed. Princeton: Princeton University Press.

Gransden, A. 1974. *Historical Writing in England, c. 550-c. 1307.* Ithaca, NY: Cornell University Press.

Grønlie, S. 2006. *Íslendingabók/Kristni saga: the book of the Icelanders/the story of the conversion.* London: Viking Society for Northern Research.

Halsall, G. 1992. "Playing by Whose Rules? A further look at Viking atrocity in the ninth century." *Medieval History* 2 (2): 2–12.

Hreinsson, V. (ed.) 1997. *The Complete Sagas of Icelanders Including 49 Tales.* 5 vols. Reykjavík Leifur Eiríksson Publishing.

Jacobsson, Á. 2005. "Royal Biography." In *Companion to Old Norse-Icelandic Literature and Culture,* ed. R. McTurk, 388–402. Oxford: Blackwell.

Larson, L.M. 1935. *The Earliest Norwegian Laws.* New York: Columbia University Press.

Lifshitz, F. 1995. "The Migration of Neustrian Relics in the Viking Age: the myth of voluntary exodus, the reality of coercion and theft." *Early Medieval Europe* 4 (2): 175–92. http://dx.doi.org/10.1111/j.1468-0254.1995.tb00066.x.

Lowe, C. 2007. "Image and Imagination: the Inchmarnock 'Hostage Stone.'" In *West Over Sea: studies in Scandinavian sea-borne expansion and settlement before 1300,* ed. B. Ballin Smith, S. Taylor, and G. Williams, 53–68. Leiden & Boston: Brill. http://dx.doi.org/10.1163/ej.9789004158931.i-614.19.

Lucas, A.T. 1967. "The Plundering and Burning of Churches in Ireland, 7th to 16th Century." In *North Munster Studies. Essays in Commemoration of Monsignor Michael Moloney,* ed. E. Rynne, 172–215. Limerick: Thomond Archaeological Society.

Lund, N. 1984. "Introduction." In *Two Voyagers at the Court of King Alfred: the ventures of Ohthere and Wulfstan together with the description of northern Europe from the Old English Orosius,* ed. N. Lund, trans. C. Fell, 5–15. York: William Sessions.

Lund, N. 1989. "Allies of God or Man? The Viking expansion in a European perspective." *Viator* 20: 45–59.

Montgomery, J.E. 2008. "Arabic Sources on the Vikings." In *The Viking World,* ed. S. Brink in collaboration with N. Price, 550–61. London & New York: Routledge.

Myhre, B. 1993. "The Beginnings of the Viking Age—Some current archaeological problems." In *Viking Revaluations*, ed. A. Faulkes and R. Perkins, 182–204. London: Viking Society for Northern Research.

Nelson, J.L. 1997. "The Frankish Empire." In *The Oxford Illustrated History of the Vikings*, ed. P. Sawyer, 19–47. Oxford: Oxford University Press.

Nelson, J.L. 2003. "Presidential Address: England and the Continent in the ninth century: II, the Vikings and others." *Transactions of the Royal Historical Society*, 6th series, 13: 1–28. http://dx.doi.org/10.1017/S008044010300001X.

Pons-Sanz, S. 2004. "Whom Did al-Ghazal Meet? An exchange of embassies between the Arabs from al-Andalus and the Vikings." *Saga-Book* 28: 5–28.

Price, N. 2002. *The Viking Way: religion and war in late Iron Age Scandinavia*. Uppsala: Dept. of Archaeology and Ancient History.

Reuter, T. 1985. "Plunder and Tribute in the Carolingian Empire." *Transactions of the Royal Historical Society*, 5th series, 35: 75–94.

Sawyer, P.H. 1962. *The Age of the Vikings*. London: E. Arnold.

Sawyer, B., and P. Sawyer. 1993. *Medieval Scandinavia: from conversion to Reformation circa 800–1500*. Minneapolis: University of Minnesota Press.

Sigurðsson, G. 2004. *The Medieval Icelandic Saga and Oral Tradition*, trans. N. Jones. Cambridge, MA: Milman Parry Collection, Harvard University Press.

Simek, R. 2004. "The Emergence of the Viking Age: reasons and triggers." In *Vikings on the Rhine: recent research on early medieval relations between the Rhinelands and Scandinavia*, ed. R. Simek and U. Engel, 9–21. Vienna: Verlag Fassbaender.

Smyth, A.P. 1999. "The Effect of Scandinavian Raiders on the English and Irish Churches: a preliminary reassessment." In *Britain and Ireland 900–1300: insular responses to medieval European change*, ed. B. Smith, 1–38. Cambridge: Cambridge University Press. http://dx.doi.org/10.1017/CBO9780511495625.002.

Swanton, M. 2000. *The Anglo-Saxon Chronicles*. New ed. London: Phoenix Press.

Wallace-Hadrill, J.M. 1976. "The Vikings in Francia." In *Early Medieval History*, 217–36. New York: Barnes & Noble (The Stenton Lecture, University of Reading, 1974).

Wolf, K. 2004. *Daily Life of the Vikings*. Westport, CT, & London: Greenwood Press.

INDEX